In Search of Belief

JOAN CHITTISTER

LIGUORI/TRIUMPH
LIGUORI, MISSOURI

DEDICATION

This book is dedicated to Mary Lou Kownacki, OSB, a sister in spirit and longtime friend, who urged me to write this book and because of whose belief my own is stronger, deeper, freer.

Published by Liguori/Triumph
An imprint of Liguori Publications
Liguori, Missouri
www.liguori.org

Library of Congress Cataloging-in-Publication Data

Chittister, Joan.
    In search of belief / Joan Chittister. — 1st ed.
    p.   cm.
    ISBN 0-7648-0337-9
    1. Apostles' Creed.   2. Christian life.   I. Title.
BT993.2.C495   1999
238'.11—dc21   98–27726

Copyright 1999 by Joan Chittister
Printed in the United States of America
08 07 06 05   10 9 8

In Search of Belief

CONTENTS

I BELIEVE...

The New Fire flamed in the blackness of the chapel. The cantor's voice spun one of those high, clear *Exultets* through the night that sounds as if it came from another world and pierces the commonness of this one. The holy water stood gleaming in the crystal font. "Do you believe in God?" the presider intoned. The solemnity of the moment demanded a special kind of attention. As he began the renewal of the baptismal promises that are an ancient part of the Easter liturgy, the relic of a time when creeds were more a private act than the signature of an institution, the questions seemed more personal than usual. Year after year it had always been the same. Year after year I had done it automatically. But this Easter night was different. "Do you believe?" I asked myself. It was the year my mother died. Her grave was still fresh in the ground, her voice still fresh in my heart. But gone. "Do you believe?" I asked myself. "Do you? Really? And if so, what?" The answer was neither a simple one, nor a simplistic one. It had been hard won, still forming, always new.

When the Christian assembly stands together to say the Creed these days, I still say "I believe" with everybody else, but I say it knowing that I believe quite differently now than I did in years past. As a result, I am convinced, the faith that lives in me now is a more demanding, more robust variety than it was in the earlier stages of my spiritual life. It is also a far less certain kind of faith and, therefore, I think, a great deal more real than when I believed the unbelievable. I used to believe, for instance, that the apostles themselves wrote the Apostles' Creed. They didn't. I used to believe that every statement in the Creed was "fact," in the sense of being provable, historical, "real." It isn't. I used to believe that God was male. Impossible. I used to believe a lot of things that I no longer believe; so do I have faith or not?

When it is at its best, religion offers more than a list of answers designed to resolve the unanswerable; it tenders a way to deal with the questions that plague our lives and puzzle our hearts. I know the transition from certainty to faith, from faithful answers to faithful questions. I have gone through it myself. So when I pray, I still say "I believe," but the truth is that I now believe both a great deal less and a great deal more than I did years ago. I believe a great deal less about the historical or scientific dimensions of the faith and a great deal more about the mystery of creation, the ongoing struggle of redemption, and the commonplace of sanctity. And furthermore, I believe that just about everybody else does, too. How in fact do we "believe"—meaning take as "fact"—a Creed even the name of which is incredible. It is, of course, pure myth that each of the apostles wrote "The Apostles' Creed."[1] What is not myth is that the Creed carries the ideas and understandings, the concepts and visions of life that underlie Christian spirituality. These are the convictions for which the apostles gave their lives to pass on to the Christian community. The ideas changed in form and purpose from age to age to suit the questions and cultures of the time, yes, but the essence of them remained: There is a God; Jesus is the Way; the Holy Spirit lives in each of us. Those are the givens, the things that do not change. But the world around us shifts like a glacier in sunlight. Now, in our time, we have again a culture in flux and questions in embryo—different from ages before us, perhaps, but no less faithful in their asking.

The question does not lie with whether or not the Creed is believable. The Creed is about the mystery of life, and its mystery is apparent. The question is whether or not the Creed is meaningful to us, here, now. Clearly, the quandary is that we live in a desert between two places, one a relatively static world where doubt was little tolerated, the other a world exploding with information, inundated with questions, where we are now and find ourselves, as a result, no longer sure.

In an era of spaceships and microprocessors, of laser beams and satellites—the stuff of science fiction and Buck Rogers comic books come to life—we talk without end about technical and cultural changes. At the same time, we talk very little about the spiritual implications of such things, or the fears they touch in the center of us, or the once commonplace theological images they shatter. Twenty years ago, in fact, Russian cosmonauts reported that they saw no heaven in the cosmos, no God on a cloud. We groped to reconcile ancient spiritual images with raw science. We struggled to adjust to a concept of space that was, it seemed, only space after all. When the Hubble telescope showed the world a universe of galaxies, the notion that the earth whirled unique in an empty void of rock-hard stars died once and for all. Surely, surely, the heart demands in the face of planet after planet, galaxy after galaxy alight on every tiny television screen before us, there must be someone else out there in that great celestial abyss. There must, too, be the Life of life who was there long before we came to know the God of the apostles, long before humanity.

As I sat and watched the news one night, Chicago physicist H. Richard Seed announced to the public that he intends to clone a human being within the next eighteen months. By the millennium, in other words, with a sheep, a monkey, and a calf to prove the possibility of the process, the whole definition of life will be in question. We find ourselves on the brink of a world full of designer people where once we saw only the hand of a creating God. What are we to believe in the face of such cataclysmic changes?

Television came alive with the subject. Programs debating the efficiency, the technology, the efficacy, the morality of cloning human beings appeared on every network. Local news programs made jokes about it. Public television programs did serious discussions. Everybody everywhere talked for weeks about the specter of duplicating ourselves scientifically. Within a week of the announcement three panelists—the reporter from the *New York Times* who broke the story of the cloning of Dolly the sheep, a biotechnologist from a national research laboratory, and a gynecologist who works with infertile couples—discussed for living room consumption on PBS's *Charlie Rose* show what till the day before Seed's announcement had been largely confined to graduate school seminars on biogenetics. They all had different opinions about the subject, of course, with one exception. On one point they were all agreed. They all took the idea for granted. They all pronounced that it can assuredly be done. They all believe that eventually—next year, five years from now, in the next ten years, at most—this procedure, which only a few months before was confidently pronounced to be totally impossible, would certainly be accomplished. Cloning, the conception of a human being's identical twin by the duplication of a donor cell, has become a commonplace in the human mind. The panelists' only question was when and how and under what restrictions, if any, it would happen. "So what will determine the acceptability of this procedure?" Charlie Rose, the PBS program moderator, asked. The question was an oblique reference to committees created in the past to determine who does or does not qualify for organ transplants. "Well, not religion," Gina

Kolata, the reporter, said. "I was there the day the President's commission called a rabbi and a Catholic priest to testify, one after the other, on the theological admissibility of such a procedure. They both used the same passage of Genesis to demonstrate their points: 'This text,' the priest said, 'proves that God does not want cloning.' And the rabbi who testified next said of the very same Scripture, 'This text proves that God has no problem whatsoever with cloning.' No consensus there," the reporter concluded.

Working at the desk while the program droned on, I was suddenly focused on the issues. I stopped slitting envelopes and making lists. I contemplated the implications of the statement. There's the real question, I thought: What are we to believe in a period of major ethical differences and massive social disbelief? What are waitresses and cab drivers and young teachers and old grandparents and secretaries and accountants and parents of small children supposed to believe when all the professional believers of the world disagree? And what is belief anyway? And should anyone believe anything that isn't self-evident? Is it any longer credible, in fact, to believe in faith, to have faith in belief? Is creed even possible now?

In a period when the world is spinning off its axis and nothing looks like it did even as recently as twenty-five years ago, belief becomes an also-ran. When the planet is not the white world's private paradise anymore and life is not incontestably a male preserve alone, old assumptions fail us. When, in the face of a possible nuclear holocaust and the rape of the earth and the obscene poverty of whole peoples, sin is obviously more than simply a social checklist of personal peccadillos, it is time to reconsider what life is really all about. It is time to ask ourselves again what it is in which we believe. It is time to retrieve the faith that underlies the rituals and to revive the sense of mystery that underlies answers that no longer persuade. It is time to reassess our place

in the world. It is time to believe in more than ourselves.
But believe in what? And how? And why?

It is a dangerous time spiritually, solved by some only
by dismissing everything that once they accepted unques-
tionably and now find incompatible with present reality or,
conversely, by others by continuing to cling blindly to past
explanations because present situations are more than they
can absorb or integrate into an older world-view. Both responses are understandable but both are lacking something
of the breadth and depth of life. One shuts out the mystical
in favor of the obvious; the other shuts out reality and calls
such anemic retreat from creation the spiritual life. The rest
of us, too cautious, too judicious, to take either extreme,
find ourselves adrift and alone, trying to make a spiritual
raft out of the shards of shattered reason. We flounder and
we drift. We avoid questions and doubt answers. We hope
against hope that someday things will all get clear again,
even while we know down deep that if life continues on its
maddeningly fascinating scientific way, more than likely they
will not. For appearances sake, we try to look as if nothing
has changed, knowing that everything has changed. We simply go on going on. But not all.

"Some people in the group said they aren't going to
church anymore," the discussion leader reported to the assembly, "because they can't say the creed with integrity. They
simply don't believe those things now." The comment has
become standard. In group after group everywhere someone sidles up to me to confess their inability to confess the
faith. Everywhere the problems are the same: Men say that
the Creed doesn't make "sense." Women say it's insulting.
It excludes the feminine from the spiritual equation of life,
a woman told me, so why believe—in the name of religion—
something that does not believe in women for what it calls
religious reasons. The situation is fraught with danger, both
intellectual and spiritual. On the one hand, it seems we are

being asked to fly in the face of the obvious. On the other hand, we find ourselves without the moorings of the soul. Little by little, one way or the other, the spiritual foundations of the Christian life go to powder. We know far too much and, in the knowing, find ourselves perceiving far too little. We have developed one-dimensional souls, awash in facts, bereft of the clarity of mystery.

Knowledge has outrun faith before this. We are not the first people in history to find ourselves with too much information and too little understanding. In ancient times, when Greek mythology ceased to satisfy the new commitment to the orderly pursuit of evidence, philosophers began to point out the contradictions inherent in popular theology. Who was really God if there were many gods? What kind of god, the Greeks asked, deserved to be served who dallied in the wanton destruction even of other figures said to be divine? What kind of religion was it that dealt with humanity in some kind of brutal sport? What was heaven if competition between the gods was par for the course and chaos part and parcel of godliness there? The old myths condemned themselves by their own hand. Intelligent people began to feel distant from a system that was arbitrary and incongruent. Religion reeled from the assault, and people lost heart for its explications. Philosophy emerged to provide more reasonable answers to the problems of life.[2]

Old religious ideas died a slow but painful death and the support of the people with them. Religion as the ancient Greeks had known it was dead. But where was the real error? Which was the greater errancy: the mythological explanations of life given by religion or the rational imaginings of the new purveyors of philosophical ideas? What was really right, the old myths or the new logic? In the end, after all, science and philosophy offered no more definitive answers to the great questions of life than the myths had done. So which was to be believed?

The situation, ancient as it seems, is uncannily like what we ourselves are facing. Science has made promises that science cannot keep. Disease is with us still. Chemicals meant to stimulate life diminish it as well. Everything we discover leads to more of what first we did not see. The more science knows, the less it knows. The more scientists pontificate, the more worrisome it becomes to wonder where and how they develop their own value systems. What is missing, perhaps, both to the Greeks and to us, is the realization that religion and science do two different things. One looks at life and attempts to understand it. The other looks at life and attempts to explain it. Venturing to wed the two may do each a disservice of immense proportions and render ourselves rudderless in the process. Science seeks verifiability of material processes. Religion seeks understanding of spiritual realities. Religion is not about equations; and its counterpart, spirituality, is not about knowledge. Religion is about transcendence, and spirituality is about finding meaning in the mundane. Religion seeks to bind the human to the divine, to bridge the gap between here and hereafter, to explain the unexplainable. It is not about history, not about science. We have, in fact, done religion a great disservice by attempting to absolutize what the Apostles' Creed itself allows simply to be more fundament than fact.

Social turbulence, then, is sure sign that the faith must be rethought, reinterpreted, restated in the light of present circumstances if the faith itself is to survive assault from an arena that is no real threat to faith at all. It is not the first time in history that new creeds have emerged in the light of new questions. The Council of Nicaea in 325, the Council of Constantinople in 381, the Athanasian Creed in the sixth century, even Pope Paul VI's "Credo of the People of God," published as late as 1968,[3] and multiple others all attempted at different times, in the face of different questions, to reformulate the fundamentals in ways they could be understood to that people at that time. We are, surely, in no less serious situation today. To question is not to deny. It may, in fact, be the truest type of faith a person can muster.

I don't remember exactly when I first began to notice the shift of circumstances, the change in attitudes, but I do know that every day the truth of the difference between past and present religious evolutions got more and more clear for me. What has for long years been considered "dissent" in the churches by those who want more answers than questions, more clerical authority than spiritual investment may not be real dissent at all. People are not challenging Christianity and leaving the Church. They are not arguing against the need for a spiritual life. They are not denying God, Jesus, the Holy Spirit. They are not ridiculing religion and going away. On the contrary. People currently considered "excommunicated" or "suspect" or "heretical" or "smorgasbord" believers are, in many ways, among the most intense Christians of our time. They do more than sing in the choir or raise money for the parish center or fix flowers for the church. They care about it and call it to be its truest self. They question it, not to undermine it, but to strengthen it. They call for new ways of being church together. They do not dismiss the need for the spiritual life. They crave it. What's more, they look for it in their churches. But they crave more than ritual. They crave meaning. They look for more than salvation. They look for authenticity and the integrity of the faith.

They do not believe in a God who tortures people for the sake of saving them from the world God created for them to enjoy. Women, in particular, find themselves with theological questions that will not go away and immerse themselves in the struggle to bring the churches to be what churches say they are. Men grapple to reconcile what the institution teaches with what the institution does. These men and women do not abandon the spiritual life, however distant their association with the churches that feel so distant from them. If anything, they try harder to provide for themselves the kind of fullness of the spiritual life their churches fail to provide or even deny, for whatever reason. They reach out everywhere to everything that will provide new insights, new awareness of the presence of God.

The women join women's spirituality groups and look for books that give them hope and teach their daughters what they themselves did not know about the gifts and graces and great good works of the women who went before them—despite eons of theological and legal restrictions arrayed against them. Men make retreats and find their way to Bible study groups and become involved in community service projects to find in the gospel what is too often lacking in the institution. Indeed, the reality is that men and women with new questions about old issues and old questions about new issues are calling the churches to be more intent on spirituality and less intent on catechisms than ever before. These are the people who identify with the tradition more than they do with the institution. These are the people who are calling the Church to bring the best of the tradition to challenge the best of the institution. They do not question because they reject the Church. They question the Church because they love it. They question because they seek a spiritual life, with or without an institution, and even outside of it if being in it is what makes the spiritual life impossible for them.

Once upon a time religion was simple and spiritual practices were the coin of its sincerity. People did what churchmen said to do, thought what churchmen told them to think, and lived controlled lives of private devotion in denominational ghettoes. Religious chauvinism made denominational religion a team sport. Our side was true; their side was false. We had the answers. They were wrong. Holy Wars were the national pastime. The world has changed its mold and hue.

Now we live in countries where Christian governments practice genocide and Muslims model great virtue, where blacks are holy and whites are godless, where true and false, right and wrong, know no single color, no one creed, no clerical status. Now we see that there are many faces of God, and each of us sees a different profile. Now religion is the question of the age and spirituality is its deepest measure.

We want more from religion now than rules. We want something to help us find meaning in life when all the rules cease to make sense, when all the old systems break down or fade away. We want a glimpse of God here and now.

The discrepancy between the obvious and the mysterious is not simply a source of institutional conflict, religious wars, and credal clashes, however. Tension between what the heart knows and what the authorities say happens on the personal level, as well. It happens many times in life, in fact. It happens at all ages. It certainly happened to me. Young. Very young. I remember it to this day:

Second grade was a most exciting place to be. You learned things there. They gave you books instead of phonics charts and catechisms instead of pictures. Every day something new happened and every day it became a family event. In fact, the first subject treated every evening was always, "Well, Joan, what did you learn in school today?" I especially reveled in the opportunity to explain the intricacies of religion to my Irish-Catholic mother, who was proud of my explanations, and Presbyterian stepfather, who was more than a little wary of things Roman Catholic. They had married in the forties, before ecumenism was even a word, let alone a virtue, and the marriage itself was a miracle in those days. But one day everything went wrong.

On that particular afternoon, I did not stay to clean the chalkboards or dust the erasers or carry out the waste basket for Sister. Young as I was, I knew that it was absolutely imperative that I get home before my father came in from work so the school question would be asked outside his hearing. I had to get things straight, check things out, work things through with my mother. Just the two of us. Catholics. Alone.

I was breathless by the time I made it out of the schoolyard, down the street, over the fence, through the alley, and into the kitchen. My mother stood at the kitchen sink, her arms up to her elbows in suds, clearing away the dishes of the day in order to clean the vegetables for supper. "Well, you are certainly excited, aren't you?" she said, taking one look at my matted hair and disheveled blouse. "What did you learn in school today that has you so wound up?" I looked around the empty kitchen and breathed a little easier. We were the only ones there. "Sister said that only Catholics go to heaven," I said softly. "Oh, really?" my mother said, still working at the sink. "And what do you think about that, Joan?" she said carefully. I took a deep breath. "I think Sister's wrong," I said. "And why do you think Sister would say a thing that's wrong?" my mother pressed. "Because," I whispered slowly, "Sister doesn't know Daddy." Sister, in other words, was missing some of the evidence. I had, after all, seen the Bible just like ours that my father had been given for perfect Sunday school attendance when he was a child. I had heard his family sing hymns and saw my little cousins say prayers. Sister clearly did not know what I knew. Sister had not seen what God saw. I looked up tentatively. My mother was simply standing there, smiling at me. To this day, I can still see her look, still feel the grain of her apron against my face. She shook the suds off her hands, pulled me up close against her warm, hard stomach, and said, "That's right, darling. That's right."

What I really learned that day is that information does not change God, it changes what we think about God. I learned that there is such a thing as belief and "belief." I learned that belief is bigger than any particular moment, however defined the vision of the moment, however absolute it may seem to be. I learned that what we believe about some things affects what we believe about other things. I learned that it is not God who changes; it is we who change. That day I learned most of all that keeping the faith requires more than keeping the rules. It may be, I have come to realize, the most important thing I ever learned in second grade.

Whatever the struggle to come to terms with the questions of an age, the truth is that there is no putting down the notion of belief. "What do you believe?" I asked the new man in a discussion group. "I don't really believe in anything much anymore," he said, and then went on to tell me about the business he was starting and the Krugerrands he'd bought. I smiled a little. He clearly believed in the god of money. "What do you believe?" I asked a younger man, fresh from a college degree, not long married. "I'm taking a Bible study course," he said. "I believe that Americans are God's special people and that the man is supposed to be the head of the family." I watched him giving his wife orders as we talked. He sat, waiting to be served his supper, while she ran after two small children. His belief, obviously, was in himself and the god of entitlements. "What do you believe?" I asked a woman who had left the Church. "I believe that God made women to have the same abilities and opportunities as men have, and I'm not going to be part of anything that says otherwise." The situations made the point: Everybody believes in something. There is no such thing as an age of "unbelievers." Some believe in self-determination and some believe in God the puppeteer. Some believe that reality is a mirage and some believe that reality is all there is. Some people believe in a God of wrath, others in a God of love. But underneath all of them there is one constant: Whatever we believe at the deepest center of our being determines what we ourselves become, even when we say we believe in something else.

No one goes through life empty of belief. Each of us draws from a well of ideas that guides us from choice to choice to choice until our life becomes the sum total of each mitered one of them. Some of those ideas are borrowed. They come from authorities and stand fast, at least until tested. Borrowed ideas are somebody else's interpretation of the human story. The ideas that shape the final us, however, come the hard way. They are the attitudes, the assumptions, the concepts which, even if handed down, will, if we are lucky, have been tried by fire. Distilled from experience, these ideas burn themselves into our souls as life works its will on us until, at the end, we find ourselves to be believers pared to the core. The fringes don't matter anymore once we come to understand the big things in life: love, commitment, God, justice, Jesus.

Ideas from authority we treat with respect. Ideas from experience we regard as pearls of great price. These are the beliefs that illuminate for us our own human story in the light of the universal one. The best beliefs, surely, are those that have been tried and found consistent with the instincts of the rest of the universe who down the long corridors of time have come back again and again to the truisms of life: There is something beyond us; there is something bigger than we are that calls us on; there is a purpose to life. It is my story flashed against the screen of the human story. It is, for the Christian, my story seen in the light of the Jesus story. It is belief tested and found to be true, not scientifically but spiritually. It is not statistical, not measurable, not historical, not scientifically verifiable. It is much better than that. It is the spiritual insight that erupts out of a community tempered by tradition and in concert with the consciousness of streams of witnesses before it, even while acknowledging that within the context of the created universe the Jesus story occupies but a millisecond.

Belief is not contrary to fact. It simply transcends it. To

believe something is to know its truth not so much in our minds but in the center of our souls. We believe in goodness, for instance, because, however effective evil seems to be, it contradicts the highest aspirations of humanity. We believe in love, rather than hate, because love draws out the best in us, while hate feeds on our smallnesses. We believe in the people whose hearts we hold in our hands, whatever the situations that challenge that certainty, because we ourselves are nourished by that relationship. We believe in the spiritual because the material is simply not enough to justify the sense of the unfinishedness of life that lurks in every human heart. In sum, belief is the ability to know what we cannot see. None of our beliefs, if they are really "belief," are sure in the way that chemicals in scales are sure. Belief is sure in the way that truth is sure. It rings in our hearts like tines on crystal.

But belief is not supernatural sleight of hand designed to save us from the exigencies of life. "There are those who say in winter," the Sufi story teaches, 'I shall not wear warm clothes. I will trust in God to keep me warm.' But they forget," the story says, "that the God who made winter gave human beings the power to protect themselves from it." Belief is not fantasy. Belief is not an excuse for irrationality. Faith is not what gives us the tricks it takes to control God. Belief is a basis for personal development and a topographical map of life that signals a way through the valleys and plains, raging rivers and vast oceans of experience in which we grow. Belief makes of life more a quest than a place. Belief is not what makes it possible for us to settle down complacent in our goodness, certain that if we keep the rules we will have life without having to live it. "I went to church every week, I did everything I was told to do, I believed in God," people say. "How could this divorce have happened?" As if belief were some kind of insurance policy against life. On the contrary. Belief is what enables us to weigh our options in the light of what is really real, what is really important in life and, in the end, stay the course.

To be without belief is to lose sight not only of where we're going but why we're going there. We become confused not only about where we are now but about where, as one more human heartbeat in a sea of life, we've been. Unbelief becomes the ground of confusion, fosters a sense of meaninglessness in life, and leaves us with a feeling of bone-weary loneliness in the universe. Without belief in something greater than ourselves, answers to the questions of why we're here, what we're doing, and how we are to live fade like grey ghosts on a white horizon. Then life shrinks to the dimensions of our own petty little world. Then we become prisoners of our own small selves captured and trapped in an even smaller box. Then life becomes just one more anthill in space. Belief in God may not be provable, true, but it is hard to imagine anything more senseless than unbelief.

There is, nevertheless, a senseless kind of belief, too. There is a dependency that masks as faith. This kind of belief thrives on absolute answers to the absolutely unanswerable, demands proofs for the unprovable, traffics in magic rather than mystery and calls it Christianity. This is the kind of religion that sets out to control God. Masked as virtue, it conjures up rules and regulations, admissions policies, and trials by fire to measure a person's right to heaven. It binds God to our laws and confuses being correct with being holy. It makes God as small as we are. It copes by convincing itself that it is possible to achieve perfect security by manipulating the cosmos. It uses God as a crutch for living. I know that kind of faith. I've been there. I collected indulgences, too.

The weakness in a spiritual life that rides on rules and regulations, definitions and doctrines is that it knows only as much of God as authority defines for it. People who rely only on predigested answers know the rituals and canons of the faith, perhaps, but they may know far too little of the God who dwells within them. They look outside themselves for answers to the spiritual life and bind God to bargains that God never made. They miss the God who is everywhere. They do not really believe, protest as they might. They simply seek to exchange compulsive compliance for perfect collateral. It is a kind of spiritual insurance plan. They may practice religion but they run the risk of ignoring the God who does not exist to be bound into therapeutic service.

The truth of life is that life is not a given. We are its co-creators. The globe is in our hands. Life is at our mercy. We must be impelled by the vision that inspired it, committed to the glory that created it, and confident in the beauty that sustains it. To say "I believe" is to say that my heart is in what I know but do not know, what I feel but cannot see, what I want and do not have, however much I have. To say "I believe" is to say yes to the mystery of life.

IN GOD...

God is the mystery nobody wants. What people covet in God is not mystery but certainty. God is what everyone seeks to be sure about. And is not. "How do you know that God exists?" the wise old professor asked the new college class at the beginning of the term. And then, impatient with the anxious silence of young people shifting nervously in their seats, looking in other directions to avoid the question, whispering back half-formed answers from faraway religion classes in Catholic grade schools, barked back, "The truth is: You don't know that God exists. No one really *knows* that God exists. You only surmise it." The word went through me with a jolt. Surmise? About God? Impossible. I remember the plaguing consternation. We must know there is a God, I insisted to myself. He'll tell us the real answer tomorrow. But no, the next day he made the question even clearer. The bad news was that there was no way to prove the existence of God. The good news was that there was also no way to prove that God did not exist. The light dawned: All our lives we had functioned on a probability. Arguments persisted on both sides of the question, of course—many of them impelling. We cannot, he pointed out, see God. But at the same time, we do see a world, a universe, for which we cannot otherwise account without positing the idea of God.

The situation became disarmingly evident: All the arguments, all of them, both for and against the existence of God, rested on speculation alone. All of them were mental constructions without a shred of verifiable data to confirm either position. There was not so much as a scintilla of hard evidence, one way or the other, from which to draw the firm conclusion that there is certainly a God. God, in other words, was a mystery. God, it seemed, was a choice.

I was astounded. How was it that God would leave Godness a question. Why, if there really was a God, would God do that? If I were God, I certainly would not have done such a thing. Nor, to tell the truth, do I know anyone else who would do it either. Everyone I know is more than quick to stake claims and leave footprints for history to embroider with praise. Why not God? One thing and one thing only answers the question: life. Life teaches us, sometimes the hard way, that what is obvious to the human soul does not demand scientific verification. Life teaches us that there are other kinds of proofs beyond test tubes and telescopes. Love is not weighable but we believe in it. Compassion is not graspable but we look for it. Fidelity is not sketchable but we see it. So, given a choice between believing in God and not believing in God, why not believe in God? It takes very little living, after all, to figure out that the God who cannot be seen is with us in darkness, that the God who cannot be touched is the only explanation for the mainsprings that drive our lives, that the God who is not containable is contained in everything. We learn, if we live long enough, thoughtfully enough, that God is not death, true, but that out of each and every loss comes a new glimpse of God. We come to realize that God is not nature, but beauty beyond measure rages in every desert sandstorm. We begin to realize that God is not people, but God visits us daily in the touch of the other.

To say "I believe in God," then, is to say to the world at large that I am steering by a star I cannot see but which I am convinced is there because I feel that it must be. The mind boggles at the intellectual poverty of the position. On the other hand, the spirit soars. What kind of a God is it who needs to "prove" anything that the human heart already clearly contains. We do not, each of us singly, fabricate out of new cloth the idea of God. We are born to it. We inherit it. I am not alone in my uncertain certainty. There is, after all, not a people in the history of the world who have not stood at the same spiritual juncture as I and not made the same choice. We know the unknowable with piercing clarity when, alone in life, we feel that only God stands by.

I can believe in God or not believe in God, yes. But there is a price for the choice.

Not to believe in God is to believe only in myself and what I see around me. Without a God, I am God. I make myself the god of my own world. I worship gods of my own making—money, power, prestige, approval, things. I insist that I will worship nothing I cannot see, and so instead I worship all the things I do see, with all their limits, all their limitations, and all the limiting they do to the expanse of my soul. It is a sorry sight. It is an even skimpier definition of humanity. Without God, human dignity itself is in danger. What else imbues human life with value, what else confers on a person an inalienable dignity, if not the fact that they, too, if there is a God, are more than they seem? No God, no meaning. No God, no purpose. No God, no cosmic quality about us at all. We are simply sand flowing through a corruptible hourglass.

In the long light of human history, then, it is not belief in God that sets us apart. It is the kind of God in which we choose to believe that in the end makes all the difference. Some believe in a God of wrath and become wrathful with others as a result. Some believe in a God who is indifferent to the world and, when they find themselves alone, as all of us do at some time or another, shrivel up and die inside from the indifference they feel in the world around them. Some believe in a God who makes traffic lights turn green and so become the children of magical coincidence in a world crying out for clear-eyed shapers of the clay we have been given in order to construct a life of value. Some believe in a God of laws and crumble in spirit and psyche when they themselves break them or else become even more stern in demanding from others standards they themselves cannot keep. They conceive of God as the manipulator of the universe, rather than its blessing-Maker. They project onto God humanity's own small needs.

I have known all of those Gods in my own life. They have all failed me. I have feared God and been judgmental of others. I have used God to get me through life and, as a result, failed to take steps to change life myself. I have been blind to the God within me and so, thinking of God as far away, have failed to make God present to others. I have allowed God to be mediated to me through images of God foreign to the very idea of God: God the puppeteer, God the potentate, God the persecutor make a mockery of the very definition of God. I have come to the conclusion, after a lifetime of looking for God, that such a divinity is a graven image of ourselves, that such a deity is not a god big enough to believe in. Indeed, it is the God in whom we choose to believe that determines the rest of life for us. In our conception of the nature of God lies the kernel of the spiritual life. Made in the image of God, we grow in the image of the God we make for ourselves.

They told us that God was creator and judge. They drew pictures to prove the point. They forgot to tell us what they could not draw. They neglected to tell us that God is both what we cannot think and what we cannot not think at the same time. We have, of course, in our attempt to understand God as personal configured the Godhead to be a person writ large and seen in that conception both the best and the worst of ourselves. Until I discover the God in which I believe, I will never understand another thing about my own life. If my God is harsh judge, I will live in unquenchable guilt. If my God is Holy Nothingness, I will live a life of cosmic loneliness. If my God is taunt and bully, I will live my life impaled on the pin of a grinning giant. If my God is life and hope, I will live my life in fullness overflowing forever. The professor was right, but he was also wrong. We cannot think "God." Irony of ironies, we can only know God.

The God-question leaves us standing at the summit of the mountain of faith facing the mountain of life. To say "I believe in God" determines the rest of our entire lives. "I believe"—"in God" may be the two most developmental statements in the human lexicon. To say "I believe in God" means that I commit myself to make God a presence in the center of my heart, in the humdrum of my days, in the dregs of my struggles. Discovering the way God works in each of those is the spiritual journey of a lifetime. It is the ultimate spiritual task. It is the quest for the Holy Grail that is buried in recesses of my own life.

THE FATHER...

One of Hinduism's holy books, the *Mahabharata*, celebrates what Hindus call "The Thousand Names of Vishnu." Among the names of God, the *Mahabharata* says, are the Creator, the Giver of Peace, the All-Knowing, the Inexhaustible Treasure, Being, the Uplifter, Jasmine, Water Lily, Lover of Devotees, Patience, the Supreme Self, Sustainer of Life, Stealer of Hearts, Answerer of Prayers, Maker and Destroyer of Fear, Holder of the Wheel of the Cosmos, Protector, Who Enjoys the Nectar of Immortality. It is a panoply of everything the mystics of that tradition name as part and parcel of the Godhead. It is a plethora of qualities, of insights, of awarenesses about the all-encompassing nature of God. It is the kind of contemplation designed to break open the soul, to stretch it beyond itself, to make earth the stuff of which heaven is made. It is a demonstration of contemplative consciousness. It is also sound theology and good spirituality.

By naming God everything that makes God God, we come daily to see God differently, to see God wholly. More than that, by naming God the sum total of created goodness, we come to see the rest of life differently, as well. In the first place, we see God present to every distinct moment, every separate segment of life. In the second place, we come to see every distinct moment of life, every gracious mortal being around us charged with that presence. We come

23

to see every facet of life—all of them, each of them—as glints of the Divine. We get a fuller picture of God. At the same time, we get a deeper understanding of the sacredness of a creation that shares in this divinity.

When we name God fully, all of life becomes an exercise in contemplation. We touch the divine dimensions of ourselves. We see God everywhere. We feel divinity everywhere. We recognize God everywhere. And, eventually, we become what we think about. We become what we see, make holy what we touch, make sacred what we are.

In this tradition, no single name names God. The practice heightens spiritual sensitivities. The world becomes, as the poet Gerard Manley Hopkins puts it, "charged with the grandeur of God." But more than that, the practice of naming God "all of life there is" also makes theology manifest. It teaches more about the nature of God in one simple gesture than the most well-meaning emphasis on any single quality of the Divine can possibly do. Clearly, if God is really God, no one name can possibly hold all the allusions, say all the concepts, breathe in one breath all the qualities that are God. That awareness changes the way we see both God and life.

The real truth is that everything we say about God is true and, at the same time, nothing we say about God is true. God is the sum total of Godness. No single dimension engraved in gold, carved in stone, dripping with dogma can suffice for it all. Every single dimension of God, though it crystallizes our understanding of God, also limits the human understanding of God. To cling to one without proclaiming the others is to make God small.

There's a message in the *Mahabharata* for all of us, even now, even here, perhaps. In their zeal to preserve a tradition under pressure from present questions, present insights, present social consciousness, there are those in the Christian tradition who insist on absolutizing one image of God over all others, of freezing only a fleeting glimpse of one the many guises of God in place in order to maintain one quality of God by suppressing others. In their ardor to maintain a bit of spiritual history which they confuse with the totality of the past, they may well be jeopardizing some of the more important, and longer lasting, dimensions of the faith.

I remember sitting in the monastery chapel with the Hindu book in my hands, staring at the tabernacle and thinking of the litanies I'd said as a child. There God, I learned— I prayed—was key, rock, door, dove, and wind. Judaism itself, the guardian of monotheism and the foundation of Christianity, records with great detail the many faces of God. To the psalmist, God is a midwife; to Isaiah a comforting mother; in Exodus, the ultimate Being; in Haggai, a wife;[4] in Luke, a shepherd and a woman searching for a lost coin; in Hebrews, a consuming fire.[5] And even far more than these, as guaranteed in the Scriptures which sketch the living God. Most important of all, the spiritual life depends on our opening our minds to all the guises of God. Otherwise, whatever we think we know of God, we know from one aspect only. It is a serious consideration. We have a hundred names for God, too, I realized. I also realized how difficult it was to use them.

In 1976 the problem finally erupted for me. Sitting in a woman's religious community, praying three times a day without a man in sight, I noticed that never once did we address a word to women. We prayed every day for our "absent brethren." We listened to prayers that called us "sons of God." We read Scriptures that told us that Jesus came to save all "men." I began, almost silently at first and then more and more loudly until I could be heard quite plainly, to change the male language as I went along. A fine young Sister, intelligent, educated, thoughtful, came to my pew one day at the end of Mass. "Joan," she said, "I know the language we use is wrong but these things take time. We have to do this carefully," she said softly, "or people will be very upset." Good idea, I thought. "Is two thousand years tippy-toe enough for you?" I said. The next week the liturgy committee began the arduous task of changing prayers drenched in maleness to include the whole human race. Now, years later, universal language is finally beginning to emerge slowly everywhere. But the struggle goes deep. So long have we made half the human race invisible that seeing them even in language is intolerable to many.

In recent times, however, confronted by the feminist concern for the theological as well as social implications of a partialism that makes God male, there is a movement growing in the Church to use sexist language for God less and less, if at all. What is self-evident theologically remains unacceptable to many, however. Jesus called God "Father," the traditionalists insist. And that must surely be true. But not only. Jesus was a Jew, and Jews obviously thought of God as many other things besides the "daddy" image used by Jesus. In a culture that stressed legalism, and a period that featured a thundering deity, Jesus' use of the term "Abba," the loving parent image for God, broke open the current understandings of the relationship between the human and the Divine to stress the intimacy of God with humanity. In the Gospel of Mark, the first recorded account of the life of Christ, Jesus uses "father" as a reference to God four times. In the Gospel of John, the last of the gospels to be written some seventy years later in an age of Roman patriarchy, God is referred to as "father" 101 times.[6] Obviously, the farther away the Church got from Jesus, the more patriarchal its language became again, not because Jesus was patriarchal, but because we are. Of course God is "father"; but God is much more than that. "God," clearly, is a very complex concept. To say otherwise is to come very close to denying belief in God.

The problem with the Creed for those whose belief in

God is whole is not that God is father. The problem is that God is not only father. To use father-language alone to demonstrate the nature of God betrays the very God we believe in. The language limps. The language misleads. The language diminishes.

The language, ancient documents say quite clearly, was very well-intended. But it was wrong. Life, a pre-scientific age assumed, came out of male semen and was simply nourished by the female womb, no ovum involved, no female life force included. If God was Creator, then, God must be male. Or, at very least, males were more like God than females were. If life was the concept to be proclaimed, then only male language made the proper point. No need for a feminine principle. No call for a feminine image. What was important in the creeds of those times, in other words, was to attest that God was life force, origin, begetter, creator, and personal progenitor of us all. God knew us; God wanted us; God cared about us and God would provide for us, the Creed implied in one single word. God was not indifferent to the human race. It was a very neat, very proper image in a patriarchal world whose science was deficient but whose theology was sound.

A language intended in the scientific climate of the fourth century to preach a personal God, however, began, someplace along the way, to present a God who is a person. A male person. Only now are the implications of that slippage clear. This language makes the perfect God human. It warps and distorts and blocks the very beauty it sets out to proclaim, that God loves what God created. In fact, by excluding the female life force from the image, it reads to many as if it were saying just the opposite—that God loves, values, "embodies" men but not women, that the fullness of life is male. If the idea were not so ungodly in its reduction of Godness to maleness, it would be funny.

I don't say, "I believe in God the 'father'" anymore, as a

result. I say that I believe in "God, our loving creator." Why? Because the Church, the best of the tradition, has taught me that. I cannot allow myself to do less and run the risk of eroding the faith, ironically enough, one prayer at a time. The fact is that contemporary concern about the use of male language for God has nothing to do with the aggrandizement of femaleness. It has something to do with praise of a God who is more than any one name we use to make this God present to our hearts.

Indeed, we need to learn to listen to the voice of God through the voice of women. I believe in that. We need to recognize the beauty of a God whose presence is relationship. Without relationships none of us can possibly come to wholeness. I believe in that. And we must expand our vision of God or find ourselves in theological decadence, in pious paganisms posing as Christianity. I believe in that to the inner recesses of my soul. But most of all, we must listen carefully to the fourth-century catechetical lecture of Saint Cyril of Jerusalem, who tells us: "This alone will be a sufficient incentive to piety, to know that we have a God, a God who is one, a God who is, who is eternal, who is ever the same...who is honored under many names."[7]

More than fifteen years later, after saying many names for God at community prayer in a monastery chapel, I found myself at a parish Mass one day, where every reference to God in every prayer, every hymn and every reflection was to God as "father." It was a shocking return to an unbelievable age. I knew in an instant that I no longer believed in that, and I was glad. Someplace along the line, almost unaware, I had, despite myself, grown a bit, I thought. But it wasn't until I found myself with a six-year-old that I understood exactly how and why.

It didn't happen in one step. At least three separate incidents brought me to this point where I felt compelled to match my behavior to my theology. The first situation occurred in the late sixties, but I haven't forgotten it yet. The night their mother died I was one of the people who undertook to get her six-year-old twins ready for bed. As each child ran down the hall fresh from his bath, he was rubbed down, bundled into pajamas, and held against the fright that comes from being without a mother. For the adults in the house it was a sad and empty night. For the children it was a time for thinking, for explaining, for understanding why and where and how things were now. Jimmy, the first twin out of the tub, was sitting on my knee waiting for his brother. "Well," he said, fresh from first grade catechism class and looking up pensively at the crucifix, "by this time Momma's in God's stomach." I felt my religious sensibilities lurch a little. "No, no, Jimmy," I corrected him, "not God's stomach, God's arms. Momma's is in God's arms now," I taught clearly and firmly. "God's arms?" Jimmy repeated, surprised and even a little chagrined, I thought. "Of course, Jimmy," I went on, repeating the old images, reinforcing half a consciousness of the nature of God. Then, finally, moved by his incredulity, I couldn't stand it anymore. I was fascinated. "Jimmy," I asked in the kind of gingerly way you use to call rabbits, "why ever would you think that mommy is in God's stomach?" "Well," the little boy answered with great certainty and patient logic, "Sister says that God is all around us. And God's stomach is the only place that I can think where you can be if God is all around you." At that moment I began to understand the power of the term "the womb of God." The concept affected me deeply that night and it affects me even more now.

As the years went by, Jimmy finally got educated beyond pristine reason. Schooled and shaped and restricted by years of narrower images of God, he took on the masculine names for God—King, Lord, Father—and became quite orthodox, quite limited in his thinking about creation, about the Divine, just like the rest of us, I'm sure. I, on the other hand,

was never able to forget his less patriarchal, far more theological revelation to me about the nature of God. It was a
six-year-old who first taught me to think of She Who Is.

In the second instance, I found myself doing graduate
work in Communication Theory at the very moment in academic history when philosophers, semanticists, and psycholo-
gists began to agree that thought does not shape language,
language shapes thought. The words I use, in other words,
determine the thoughts I think—about myself, about the
world, about life and all its relationships, including my relationship with God and God's relationship to us. The
thought began to burrow into my soul like grass cracking
cement. Who was this male God, I wondered, who created
women but wanted nothing to do with them, except of
course at a subservient distance? Six-year-olds, I began to
discover, are dangerously close in mentality to university
professors. Or vice versa, perhaps.

Finally, at Call to Action, the great assembly of the
Church held in Detroit in 1976 as part of the plethora of
activities scheduled to coincide with the bicentennial celebration of the United States, I was on the quiet, unnoticed,
pathetically small, seven-person subcommittee on language
that emerged out of the section on "Women in Church and
Society." The other two hundred or so delegates in that particular segment of the conference were in subcommittees,
concentrating on far weightier matters. They wanted Church
commissions on the status of women, the theological justification for the ordination of women, the social equality of
women, the political involvement of women at the highest
levels of organizational life. No one paid much attention to
the idea of language as an item of major importance to the
issue. No one paid much attention to us at all. I predicted to
the small group dedicated to the subject of language in liturgy, in fact, that every other recommendation but ours
would pass without protest in the General Assembly but

that ours on inclusive language would be a struggle all the way. The committee laughed a little at the thought. Who could possibly agree to the ordination of women and question the use of two pronouns for the human race and the emphasis on the purely spiritual nature of God as distinct from the androcentric notion of a male God in a patriarchal Church? The laughing did not last very long. One after another of the proposals passed easily. The fury broke out over the call for nonsexist language in liturgy. Clearly, the Christian community, entrenched in a bad biology that had become the theology of the Church, knew intuitively that the real revolution started with pronouns, not with proposals for ordination.

This reluctance to broaden, change, complete the image of God by moving beyond fatherhood—as if "fatherhood" were the sole element of creation, as if semen were the only raw material of the human race and women merely its incubators—left the human psyche deeply scarred and theology in contradiction with itself. What we taught we did not demonstrate. What we believed we did not accept. Patriarchy—the domination, oppression, ownership, and control by the fathers—became the Divine Order of the day and with it the rape of the earth and the rape of the women, as well. Then Jimmy and graduate school and an assembly locked in mortal combat over the name of the God whose name is "I am" began to come together for me in a torrent of pain, a rush of awareness, and an immeasurable depth of disillusionment with a Church that called itself "True."

The fact is that nothing will really change in the way the world goes together until we change the language, until we learn to think differently, until we learn to see women as an equal image of God and the images of God as birthing mother, loving spirit, passionate compassion, heart of justice, and womb of the universe.

No, a person does not come to this new understanding

of the relationship pointed to in the Creed from one point only. A least I did not. Experience, a developed sense of selfness, and theology all lead the way. But language, we must never fail to remember, either reveals the revelation— or obscures it.

We need language that gives us a fuller picture of the God who birthed us. Then, the world will be a softer, safer place and God a God big enough to be worthy of belief.

ALMIGHTY...

God is very close to you," my mother whispered in my ear every night as she pulled up the covers and kissed me goodnight. It had been the ritual for as long as I could remember, my last thought as day ended, my first thought at dawn. What I never told my mother was that, though I liked the thought, I had come over the years to question it a bit. The fact is that the messages were not consistent. She said one thing; everybody else said another. "God is in heaven," they had told us in catechism class. So, who was right? My mother or the books? And the rest of the messages weren't consistent, either. God is just like us, they taught us on Monday; God is like no other, they taught us on Tuesday. God is present, they said one day; God is transcendent, they said the next. God is personal; God is totally Other. Which?

The jangling of concepts shakes the soul to its roots. Who is this God exactly? Where is this God exactly? And what does being "almighty" mean in an age that has granulated two cities with two bombs, decimated a people, burned a hole in the ozone layer, and landed on the moon? Where is God in all of this destruction, all of this probing of the universe, if God is truly "almighty"? If we call God "father" to imply the poignancy of a personal relationship between the human and the Divine, where is this relationship when we need it most? Or, conversely, how is God almighty

33

if God does not act almighty when we need it. Can we possibly believe that a God who loves us intimately can possibly allow us to destroy ourselves? The answer, I have come to believe with total conviction, is yes.

I deeply believe that God is almighty. But I do not believe that God is a magic act. God is much more than that. God is almighty enough to enable me to be what I can become without having to depend on a Superman God. Clearly, when God intervenes in life, God intervenes through us, through the natural order, through the grace of conversion, through processes that may suspend the natural order of things but does not contradict them, nevertheless. Nowhere in all the miracle literature of all time do we find, for example, instances of regenerated limbs, whites who become blacks, buildings bombed to smithereens that stood untouched.

The real miracle, I believe, lies in the fact God provides us with everything we need in life to come to wholeness by living well the lives we have, however paltry they may be. If there are those who lack the goods of life, it is not because God does not provide them. It is because we do not provide them. God is not a ringmaster whose function it is to save us either from the learnings of life or from the darkest, weakest parts of ourselves. To hope otherwise, I am convinced, belies the very notion both of life and of the nature of God. Life, if we allow it, is what grooms us to the point of godliness. God is what waits to fulfill us when we have finally filled ourselves to the ready point.

To want God to make things perfect in the here and now is the talk of those who believe that the fullness of life, world, reality, truth, right, and good are the stuff of what we can see and hold and touch. It makes irresponsibility a virtue. We want interventions from God, in other words, to make the world what we want the world to be rather than to change ourselves so that the world can become what it ought to be. We want someone else to do something, rather than face the need to become something other ourselves. We want a God who does physical miracles rather than spiritual ones.

"First God created man," the wag wrote, "And then man created God." The humor lies in the truth of the statement. We want "almightiness" on our own terms. We have projected onto God our compulsion to change things, to make them other than they are, to warp, and stretch and shape them to ourselves. We want a God who does the same. "Where is God?" we say, when the world does not meet our specifications, when the horrors are more than we can grasp in a single sitting, even in a single lifetime. We rebel against the idea of God when the world does not suit us. As if we are not its microcosm. As if what we know needs to be done is not itself the mind of God at work in us. We do not see conscience as an intervention of God, though we talk about its effects. We do not accept love as an intervention of God's, though we talk about its power. We do not seek spiritual change in the world—compassion in the face of global poverty, kindness in personal relationships, justice in human interactions, patience at stoplights. We want, instead, results that will eventually go to dust. We want power, control, triumph, security, victory. We want God to be almighty so that we can be almighty.

New developments in science tell us a great deal about almightiness. They tell us that things are more than they seem to be, that physical reality is simply a chimera, a mask for the invisible labyrinth of life that underlies it, a container for the energy that electrifies a dynamic universe. There is no such thing as solid matter, scientists in an age of electrons tell us. Everything is made up of particles of electric energy, each of them living, all of them always in motion which when one form is destroyed it will become another. The world of material and nonmaterial objects blurs in this new view of physics. We are all, at base, the same now. We are all, at base, eternal. What is almighty, in other words, is not what we see; it is what we do not see. God is above us, beyond us, within us, around us, and beside us. What can possibly be more "almighty" than that. What almightiness do we possibly need more?

To look for proof of God in things beyond the "natural" seems to me to be its own kind of heresy. The point is that we know more and more and less and less every day about what is "natural." To the primitive mind, lightning and fire, flying through the air, and talking through space were not "natural." For us they are. We call them electricity and gas stoves, planes and telephones. There is no reason, in other words, to demand a God who does tricks in life. There is more than enough almightiness in the universe as we know it and discover it and feel it to remind us daily of the miracle of being alive. There are signs of God's power— the definition of "miracles"—everywhere. Some of them can be accounted for; some of them cannot. But who cares? That we can explain them does not diminish the wonder, the potency of them. The only thing that can do that is us.

The other miracles of life—peace and sobriety, care and compassion, self-development and other-centeredness— come from within ourselves. When those things die, it is because we have not enabled them to live. The obvious disturbs us: God does not exist to save us from our ourselves. What humans created—nuclear weapons, drugs, marauding armies, houses of prostitution, sexism, racism, hunger, and poverty—humans can refuse to develop, refuse to have, refuse to use, refuse to support, refuse to ignore. Those would be miracles, too.

Living life to its fullness—whatever life is for us—makes the Almighty real. Otherwise Helen Keller's mute-deaf life was useless, Franklin Delano Roosevelt's paralysis was destructive of him as a person, Martin Luther King, Jr.'s blackness rendered him powerless, Virginia Woolf's femaleness disproved her intelligence. In every case, God wills more for us than the world expects. In every case, the power of God makes what the world calls imperfect perfectly right for us. Whoever made "almighty" and "perfect" synonyms missed the almightiness of God completely. Recognizing that whatever remains in life when we have done everything in our power to prevent it, represents the beginning of another miracle. Believing that God is working with almighty love and almighty power in our own life, however painful the present, however much our need to change what must be changed, carries us beyond our dense and common selves to immersion in the energy that is God. The point is not that God is not almighty. The point is that to see the Almighty God we must wrest ourselves open to the almightiness of God in us, around us, beneath us, before us, in every possibility that impels us to be more than we are.

I have seen miracles aplenty: people cured who lived to die another day; people deeply depressed who held on to life until they found something else to laugh about; people who wanted what they could not have and learned to love what they had been given. What could be more almighty than that? I know because I have been there.

My mother lived with Alzheimer's disease for at least twenty-eight years before she died. Or at least that's when I first began to realize that something was terribly wrong with her. "The woman you know," I told a friend in the midst of my confusion, "is not the woman who raised me." First, she lost the bubble of her laugh and the balance in her personality, then little by little she lost her emotional control, then slowly, slowly she lost her sharp, stiletto-like mind, then finally she lost her speech. Was her life useless? Where was Almighty God then? The answer became more clear every day of those twenty-eight years. The almighty power of God was in the rest of us who gave her the care, the security, the attention she needed even when she could not give it back. She brought us all to be better people. God was clearly almighty still. Intrusive, no; almighty, yes.

It is not difficult to believe in the almightiness of God once we stop defining almighty on our own terms, once we come to the point in our life where we allow God to be God, where we allow God to work through us.

In the meantime, I pray, "I believe—in God—the creator—almighty" knowing that God is being as almighty in me as I have finally mustered the courage to allow and been given the opportunity to attempt. And for now, at least, that will have to be enough.

5

CREATOR...

A s I grow older, I become more and more fascinated by the fact that we teach to children what adults do not understand. I have also come to think that this is just exactly the way it should be. "Who made you?" the catechism asks children. "God made me," the catechism answers. The response may be disarmingly simple, if not simplistic, but the topic is not a contrived one. On the contrary. The question, constant and common, emerges early in the human heart. "Where did I come from?" I asked my mother at about the age of three. "God sent you to us," she said back just as quickly. Case closed.

It is the most artless of answers to the most difficult of questions but, deep in the most hollow regions of human thought, what else is there to know? Except, perhaps, maybe how it all came about—the long answer to which, for most people on a daily basis, is "Who cares?" I mean, really? In the long run? From a personal point of view? At the level of the immediate, what does it matter how life came about? The fact is that we are all here by virtue, ultimately, of something beyond and greater than ourselves. We and our universe with its intelligent order, its sense of purpose, its kaleidoscopic beauty, its centrifuge of feeling, were obviously created out of something other than ourselves. We were created by a creator. An intelligent, personal, powerful creator. We may not know the manner of the process but we know the profundity of the production. We and our planet are the most perceptible proof of creation we have.

To the scientist, of course, the process matters immensely. Were we created in an instant, over billions of years, progressively or as a whole? Are we the ultimate moment of Creation or does Creation go on creating? Have we really been created once and for all or are we on our way to another stage of life yet to be seen, yet even to be imagined? Those are questions that have to do with the physical dimensions of life. Those are issues yet to be discovered, if they ever are with any kind of surety, any degree of totality. But they are not the questions raised by the Creed.

To the human soul, the real question is not who is responsible for Creation. That is clear for the simple reason that it is so unclear. We did not create ourselves. We have been created by a life force outside ourselves so strong that it can only be called God, be called Mystery, be called Being. The real spiritual question, therefore, is far more simple, far more profound than the scientific one. The spiritual question demands to know: What does this creation imply for us?

The Creed does not come to us as textbook—no matter who would like to make it one. In the Creed beats the heart of a Christian tradition that has kept the faith and changed its mind about the way it understood the workings of God in life over and over again. The Creed comes simply to remind us of who we are: creatures.

In the early Middle Ages, Christianity tried to use the science of the time to prove faith and define creaturehood and failed miserably.[8] In our own age, fundamentalists who claim that the Bible's rendering of Creation must be taken literally registered dismay, reports claim, at the fact that Pope John Paul II in a statement to the 1996 assembly of the Pontifical Academy of Science acceded that evolution is "more than just a theory."[9] For centuries Scripture and science were combined, confused, conflated. Scientists who did not conform to a literal understanding of Scripture flirted with heresy, and churchmen who called Scripture science encouraged disbelief. We learned the hard way.

We excommunicated Galileo and then had to reverse the position four hundred embarrassing years later. We rejected Darwin and now accept his premises. We hounded the paleontologist Chardin and find ourselves forced now to deal on a universal scale with the theology that emerges from his science. Clearly, faith is not another kind of science. In fact, as modern science contested and disproved one theological speculation after another, the foundations of a faith that called itself science shook to the ground. Or truer yet, perhaps, faith became faith again. Science discovered its material limits, and faith discovered its real purpose.

Science was not the business of spirituality. Though science could tell us some things about the mechanics of life it told us nothing about the purpose of life. That, we finally came to understand, was the province of faith. As a result, after centuries of dispute, we eventually discovered that faith and science are neither allies nor enemies, though each can benefit from the contributions of the other. Faith cannot disprove what science knows about matter because matter is not its discipline; and science can neither prove nor disprove what faith knows about the spirit because the spiritual has no place in a test tube. One speaks to the other, but they speak in different languages. Science drags faith beyond magic. Faith challenges science to principles beyond utilitarianism. One does not explain the other. We look in vain for faith to tell us how the world began or why it functions as it does with floods in wetlands and desertification in dry places and massacres in Algeria and pain in my own small life. But we do look for faith to tell us what it means to have to deal with such things.

When I say I believe in "the Creator," then, I am saying a great deal more about me than I am about God. I am saying a great deal more about the purpose of life than I am about the processes of life. I am saying a great deal more about what it means to be a creature than I am about what it means to be Creator.

The point of the Creed is simply that I believe that I am not God. The statement is a disarming one. Who would possibly think otherwise? Obviously intellectually false, the statement is nevertheless almost certainly operationally true. Slave masters, for instance—people who deal in the lives of others—almost certainly do. Corporations that set out to exercise monopolies of world resources and human labor and the distribution of capital clearly do. And I know in the darkest depths of my heart that I do. When I expect God to do on a universal scale what I will not do in my small wedge of the world—stop the conflicts in my heart, share the apples on my apple tree, tithe for charity, listen to another person's pain, put someone else's happiness before my own—I make myself the beginning and the end of the universe. I make myself God.

But the very act of being born brings us to moments in life far richer, far deeper than those. Learning that I am incomplete, admitting that there are things I do not know, realizing that there are situations I do not understand, dealing with the results of things I have not done well constitutes one of the rudimentary shocks of creaturehood. It can take a lifetime to come to appreciate the invitation to join the human race that recognizing my restraints brings with it. It can also leave a lifetime bare and sterile of insight unless I do. It's when I'm protecting the territory that is my godhead that I find myself mired in misery, hopelessly lost, sick with the struggles of life.

Accepting my creaturehood frees me to lean on life a little. Sooner or later, it becomes plain to me what has been plain to everyone around me for years: I do not have all the strength. I do not have all the answers. I do not have all the wealth I want. I can be wrong. I can be in pain. And, I can learn. Reaching out for help, admitting my limitations, links me to the dross, to the rabble, to the riffraff of humanity. At that point begins the glory of my mortality.

"In my weakness is my strength," Paul writes (2 Cor 12:10). I never understood that passage nor did I like it until, struck with polio as a young woman, I began little by little to realize that if I ever walked again, it would not be thanks to me, it would be thanks to everyone around me who formed the human chain that kept me human. When I could not move, they carried me. When I could not work, they found functions for me that justified my existence. When I could not find a reason for going on, they liked me enough to give me back a sense of human connectedness. When I could not cure myself, they cured me of the clay of my limits and turned them into life again. They taught me the glories of weakness for both of us. When I most of all wanted to be strong and like no other time in life found myself defined by my weaknesses, I began to understand the great question of life. If I do not need other people, what can I ever learn? And if I do not need other people, what is their own purpose in life, what is their claim on my own gifts when they need me as I have needed them? The moment I come to realize that it is precisely the gifts which I do not myself embody that make me claimant to the gifts of others—and they of mine—marks the moment of my spiritual beginning. Suddenly, creaturehood becomes gift and power and the beginning of unlimited personal growth.

But personal development is not the only by-product of a holy consciousness of creaturehood. The comprehension of human need, the awareness of human accountability also makes the massacres in Algeria and the poverty in Bangladesh both more understandable and more tragic. To expect God to stop such travesties, to wait for God to solve such sin begs the question of culpability, avoids the accountability that comes with creaturehood. We do not need God to solve such things. We do not have—as one woman sickened by the specter of an uncaring God in a globe reeking of suffering called it—"a dispassionate, impotent God" who creates us and abandons us. On the contrary, this God—the fullness of Being—has poured out in us all the feelings we need to feel such things ourselves. It is not that we are not equal to them. The fact is that we simply ignore them or avoid them or, in the name of religion, throw these things and all the responsibility for allowing them, for redressing them, back on God. We ignore the demands, the duties, the deep down daily awareness that it is we who rampage through life playing God but creating chaos where we should bring order. We have, as a people, sinned, and we can, if we want, as a people, repent and repair it.

We do not need God to do what we can do but do not. There is no need, no value, nothing to be gained by God's saving what we will not. A God who saves us from the effect of our collective sins is a God who takes away creaturehood and reduces it to toadiness, takes away human valor and changes it to robotics, takes away human dignity and makes it a joke. What's worse, perhaps, it makes God the narrator of the play called life which we ourselves rise every day to write out of the ground of Being whom we call God. Wanting God to change the world may well be the infallible sign that there is something we ourselves are failing to do. "God hears the cry of the poor," the psalmist reminds us. The psalm says not a word about God changing things, only that God "hears." And remembers. And waits for us to become more than we are. Like infants born with the potential to be adult, we are each created with the potential to become wholly human, totally mature, completely spiritual people.

Life does not come to us whole and entire. Creation, science tells us, is neither a single nor a static act. We are not complete nor is the world around us. Each of us, we and our world, are still developing. Every day we are meant to become more human. Every day we are meant to make humanity a glimpse of the Divine. Every day, finite and small, we participate in the Being that makes beings of us all. Every day we too are required to look at what we do to redeem or destroy what God called "very good." What we do, each of us in our isolated little corner of the earth, to make that happen rings across the universe like ripples in an ocean.

To say "I believe...in the creator" proclaims, out of the center of my soul, that I know that life is a gift, a responsibility, a venture into human accountability for which there is no excuse acceptable, no justification adequate enough to explain why I did nothing to complete a world given to me for safekeeping. We may, of course, fail because failure is also a mark of creaturehood, the beginning of a growth learned over and over again, from generation to generation, to the end of time. Success is, therefore, not required. We are frail, uncertain. But the outpouring through us of the Breath of God, the spirit that brought each of us into being and sustains us there, is of the essence of God's work on earth. The massacres may go on, the injustices may be legalized, the oppressions may be theologized, the barbarisms may be taken for granted everywhere, but I am expected to meet inhumanity with humanity, human darkness with the gleam of the divine eye at all times, spiritual death with the living Breath of God. I am expected to draw from the Being that is the source of my being so that all of us together may someday, somehow grow to full stature, become that from which we were made, be everything that creaturehood demands.

The Talmud teaches that every human being should wear a jacket with two pockets. In one, the rabbis say, we should carry the message, "I am a worm and not even fully human." In the other, the rabbis teach, should be the message, "For me the world was made." The awareness of creaturehood is what leads us to understand how it is that we expect so much and do so little, why we accomplish so little and attempt so much, how grand is God and how glorious the dust that breathes that Breath. Creaturehood is a quest for the Other, the pursuit of Being, the impassioned quest for the More. It is the magnet that carries us over every chasm, beyond every mountain, around every dark corner, grateful for what is and searching for what can be.

What we call perfect may not be perfection at all. It is simply life as we want it, the world as we would shape it. Real perfection may lie in dealing with the imperfect perfectly well, knowing that we are not autonomous, realizing that we are answerable, understanding that we are in a cooperative venture with the fullness of Being which, if I myself am less than I can be, may well fail.

I stood in a mud hut in a Mexican barrio. Three dirty children crawled along the floor, their bellies distended with worms, the stream below the house a running latrine. The young mother looked twice her age. She was blind in one eye, thin, living in a hovel, and bent over the old treadle sewing machine that was her only livelihood. "Marta," one of the members of the group asked suddenly, "What is your happiest moment in life?" Marta paused, crossed her arms tightly across her chest, lowered her eyes, and said softly, "Maybe when it's over."

I realized how easy it is to fool ourselves in the name of religion. I knew looking at Marta, whose creaturehood was painfully, pitifully obvious in a life where death was preferable that we had failed in our creaturehood, as well. Perhaps because we fail to understand it. We tell ourselves that our purpose in life is to seek the Divine when the Creed says quite clearly that it is to recognize the fullness of humanity and its implications for the rest of the world. That, surely, is what creaturehood is really all about. Looking at Marta, I knew without doubt that I believe in God, the creator of a creaturehood mired in flaw but destined for glory.

OF HEAVEN...

At one level it was the mistake of the day, a total waste of time, an excursion into nonsense. At another level, it was one of the best experiences I've had in a long time. Half joking, fully expecting to get very little response from the search, I went onto the Internet looking for material on the World Wide Web about "heaven." I expected to find a few articles on the origin of the word, perhaps. Certainly some theological references. Probably a collection of book titles. Maybe some biblical allusions. Hopefully an article or two about the origin and interpretation of the concept as it emerged throughout history. Instead, I found, on one search engine alone, 323,751 articles referenced under the title "Heaven." Heaven may well be one of the hottest topics on the web. And this in an age of laser beams, space stations, and glutted materialism. And why? Perhaps, given the corruption of the term over time, for that very reason. Heaven is the way a materialist insures a commitment to materialism. It becomes the depository of everything we ever wanted in life and did not get. No wonder it is difficult for reflective people to say "I believe in...heaven" with any kind of critical consideration. Heaven has become a very childish notion.

It may also be the one spiritual notion that develops very little over time. If we pursue the idea of heaven at all consciously as we get older, whatever we've learned about

47

heaven when we were young we tend to maintain, it seems. We may pass it on embellished a little, on one hand, and muted a bit on another, but, down deep, the concepts remain fundamentally the same. We turn heaven into a place of unfulfilled wishes, of unaccomplished dreams. We teach it to our children and with evangelistic fervor or sophisticated disdain either cling to it as adults or abandon the concept completely. On our notion of heaven may well rest the measure of the rest of our entire spiritual life.

Heaven becomes a psychological Rorschach test of spirituality. What we think about heaven has something to say about our entire psychological development as well as our spiritual maturity. It refracts with the accuracy of a prism the depth of the spiritual energies that drive us. For some, heaven is a reward. For others, heaven is a state of mind.

Heaven, the Christian tradition explains, is a state of perfect union with God, the proper end of a relationship with God begun in life and consummated in a way we do not know, at a time we cannot measure hereafter. Heaven is union with the Source of Life. Heaven is not adult Disneyland. It is not the wafting off to another world just like this one but free of pain and pressures and points of struggle. It is also not an excursion to nothingness. In Jewish mystical literature and in the Islamic tradition, as well, heaven is a seven-level ascent from the lowest to the highest awareness of the presence of God. In Buddhism, heaven is the extinction of the desires that plague us and eventual union with the Creator-God who is everything we need to be happy. In every major religion, then, heaven is, ultimately, immersion in the fullness of Being. To be in heaven is to be filled with the essence of everything that is. It is the end of the beginning, the final culmination of life into the Being out of which our being pours. Heaven lies in coming to fullness of life in the Breath of God that both created and sustains us.

I remember being told in the flush of young adulthood by an enthusiastic retreat director—too young himself perhaps to see that the only proper end of life was Life itself—that all we would do in heaven would be to sing "Alleluia" forever. I was not interested. Boredom was not my definition of God. How could God possibly be some sort of supernatural narcissist and be everything else that God must be? I have not changed my mind. Not if God is God. Heaven, surely, is not passive praise of a Divine Potentate. Heaven is the achievement of the peak of Being. It is total immersion in the Mystery. It is the real moment of Becoming. It is the glorious grasping of Being. It is full consciousness of Life alive within us. It is, in other words, the end of a long process which we already know even now but too, too often fail to recognize. Heaven is becoming what I am and have always been and am meant to be in full.

Heaven is not something we get, in other words; it is something we become. Heaven is something we find within ourselves, something we discover beyond ourselves, something we come to see and learn to touch and begin to feel in us and around us now. Heaven is finding God now and then growing into life always more and more. Life is not about its endpoint. Life is about making the journey to the within and the ultimate in the consciousness of where we're going.

It's not that heaven is not true. It is just that heaven is not real. Not in the sense of being a place of Unlimited Desire. It isn't that heaven won't come. It's just that heaven already exists. It's not that we won't go to heaven. It's just that heaven is already here. Theologians of every stripe call heaven "the place or state of righteous souls after death." The words elude but the concept does not. Heaven is the state of perfect immersion into God, the state of fullness of life, the state of conscious confluence with the Cosmic. Heaven is the abode of God—who not corporeal, not material, not bodily—is Being, not "place." Once we turn away from childish notions of heaven, we find it where it has always been: inside ourselves. Because God is, heaven is—like God—everywhere. A disappointed disciple, the Talmud teaches, seeing studious rabbis pouring over the Torah in a plain anteroom of heaven, asks of the angel who is conducting him through paradise, "Are those sages in heaven?" And the angel answers him, "Oh, no, friend. The sages are not in heaven. Heaven is in the Sages." When we become everything we are able to be wherever we are, we grow into heaven without even noticing it.

Heaven is, consequently, as much now as it is to come, only yet to be in full. The more we sink into God, the more we immerse ourselves in goodness, the more we become the beauty around us—the more we transform evil into good, the more we love, the less we hate—the more we have of the heaven that is here, the closer we are to heaven forever. Heaven is not a place. Heaven is a process of growing fully into the fullness of Being.

But heaven can also be defined as the most sordid of spiritual tricks designed to turn what should be spiritual adults into religious children. Used to coerce behavior with the thought of reward or punishment, heaven becomes the lowest possible level of spiritual development. It turns God, the fullness of Being, into Big Parent, Great King, Theological Cop more interested in faultless adherence to institutional requirements than in the fullest development of the spiritual person. It makes of Creation a kind of disciplinary exercise rather than the process of growth to full stature.

Living now in the womb of God, we are growing now to Life. Heaven, presented as some kind of spiritual contradiction to the life of nature, induces subservience, slavery, and egregious escapism. Anything that happens on earth, this theology argues, is the will of God which will be "rewarded" in the next life if we accept the unacceptable passively. So much for the God of Justice and a Loving Creator. This God is a tease and a bully, a sadist and a senseless sentry of a warped life. This God is not God. To find life where death resides is one thing. To accept cruel and inhuman deaths in the name of Life is another. It is this kind of religion that Marx called "the opium of the people," the spiritual drug used by unscrupulous oppressors to induce the world to accept cruel masters and mean conditions and gleeful torture with unthinking resignation.

But the heaven I believe in is far greater than that. It is a taste for the More. "The Kingdom of heaven is within you," Jesus taught. Life around me will not cease to be whatever it is, perhaps, but life within me always offers more. More depth of understanding. More of a sense of justice. More breadth of wisdom. More levels of gratitude. More layers of kindness. More grasp of God. Heaven is nothing but fullness of life and union with God. If I do not burst into heaven here, make heaven here for me, for everyone, I sincerely doubt that I will find it anywhere else. This life as I have been given it is my beaker of God who is in everything, everyone, everywhere.

Heaven is the criterion of our ideals, the measure of the awareness of Godness around us, and the appreciation of nowness become forever.

Indeed I believe that God created "heaven." I simply don't believe that heaven is the Sugarcane Land that we present it to be. It is the Stream of Life that lives and flows through me as well as through the universe. It is the best of myself calling me to be even better. I believe I have it now and can have more of it, the closer my own life gets to the Godlife.

And so I search for that God without ceasing. I search everywhere. In the cesspools of poverty that keep people from becoming fully human. In the confusions that reign in the human community as we thread our way from one insight to the next. In the uncertainties that mark the circumstances of my private life. In the great, grand miracles of human goodness and in the little gestures of a personal God so apparent in other persons. In the faces of God I see on the faces of those who love me. Am I "going to heaven"? No, I am already there and it is getting more heavenly every day. The Creed is about who we are now. It is about the God in whom we live when we die. That I believe.

7

AND EARTH...

I believe in God...the creator...of earth" may be one of
the most proclaimed—and least believed, barely prac-
ticed—assertions of all the propositions in the Creed.
In fact, religion itself has forever proclaimed the truth about
the value of Creation on one hand and taken it away on the
other. Earth, we got the impression, was a kind of divine
mistake. Its temptations delayed our sanctification. Its glories, beautiful but false, seduced us to substitute lesser things
for the real values of life. Its cycles simply reminded us of
the inferiority of our own natures. Dust we were and to
dust we would return. It pitted the material against the spiritual dimensions of life. It misled us about the purpose of
existence. It was the forbidden apple in everybody's life.

But all the messages were mixed. We were, they taught
us at the same time, sacramental people, people who celebrated and symbolized the presence of God in all of creation—in human love and fallible community, in human
birth and mortal death, in human response to good and in
superhuman resistance to godlessness. We did, after all, use
water and oil, bread and wine, candles and incense, flowers
and salt, bells and organs—things of the earth, in other
words—to summon up inside of us the blessedness of
human life and the ordinariness of divine grace. The earth,
we said, was the thunder roll of divine presence. And then
we proceeded to ignore its place in the flowering of the

human spirit and the achievement of human development. Creation loomed as a temptation to be overcome. The notion of the spirituality of creation itself seldom made its way into the spiritual manuals. Life in itself was not a channel of grace, let alone our major channel of grace, maybe our only channel of grace. No, the religion lessons were clear, God had given us a paradise but paradise was, in the end, a worthless and disappearing trap. And the sooner the better.

But I lived another life at the same time. "Never, ever, throw anything in the water," my father taught me when we were out fishing, pop bottles and sandwich wrappers all over the bottom of the little skiff. "Never, ever, throw cans out a car window," my mother warned as I finished the last of an afternoon snack in the back seat. These other messages were the descant against which I lived my young life: Don't ever hurt an animal. Don't ever keep more fish than you can eat. Don't ever use more of anything than you need. Don't waste anything. Don't ever dig up flower gardens. Don't ever trample down small trees. Don't ever hurt a baby bird. Why? Because, that's why. Because making a garbage heap out of the water and the woods, my property or nobody's property, destroyed the beauty and goodness of creation. Because destroying another being just for the sake of destroying it took life in vain. Because creation was good and each part of it had its own purpose, that's why. Because we were to walk through life on tiptoe, as part of creation, not as predators with swollen bellies and bloated souls. We were to learn from animals and care for flowers, to have enough and never too much. We were meant to leave the world better than when we found it. This was more than the kind of paltry stewardship that conserves so that we can continue to be rapacious. This was a way of life that held more than humanity sacred. Those lessons ring in my heart until this day, more loudly than ever before.

And yet, everywhere around me, they are in tension with another, equally impacting, message. "Subdue it and have dominion over it," the message of the first Creation story in Genesis 1 began, after the Industrial Revolution, to take precedence over "Till it and keep it," the command given in the version of the Creation story found in Genesis 2. The second message—the call to stewardship and the inherent connectedness of all life—marked the understanding that had so clearly shaped my parents' attitude to the world around them. The first message—the national anthem of human superiority—I picked up from religion class, from the pulpit, from the world around me. The terms of the debate were clear. We were responsible for the world, of course, but it had, after all, been made for us. It was there for the taking. Paradise was not gone. It was just a little harder to get now. We worked for our pots of gold "by the sweat of our brow." But there was no question: the pot of gold—the forests, the minerals, the air, the water, the land— belonged to anyone with enough money, power, energy, or will to wrest away the capital of creation from the treasure house of a planet rapidly falling prisoner to the political systems of the world.

"Subdue" and "take dominion over" are harsh words but far easier to understand in the context of life on earth once you have enough religion to realize that material things in a world neatly divided into categories of spirit and mat-ter are inherently temporary, essentially without value, fun-damentally seductive. The spiritual dimension, the aspect of life that is not corruptible as matter is, counts. In the end, nothing else really figures in the great equation of life. All the earth, then, and everything in it lies inert and submis-sive at our feet, and all of it simply for the sake of human comfort, all of it a veritable cornucopia of human gadgetry, all of it bangles on the human crown: great white leopards and long, thick elephant tusks, mink furs and hardwood forests. All for us. The world becomes only a stage for human activity of which we form but one part, not an ecological system, not a microcosm of God.

Worse than that, the material dimension of life, religion taught, constituted a test of spiritual will, a seduction to moral death, an enticement to be avoided at all costs, a temptation to be denied in the pursuit of sanctity. And the worst of these was, I learned as life went by, my very own body. A woman's body, most of all, like the earth around it, existed for use, for birthing rather than for thinking, a woman's brain to the contrary notwithstanding. The Creed had failed us. What they said they believed, they did not. Matter was not sacred. To those who preached a theology of domination, earth was dangerous to the human spirit and women were its human complements, made to be ruled, born only to bear human fruit, deprived of reason and required to serve.

Indeed, we have denied the Creed its prophetic dimension. Taught instrumentalism by the Church and profit by society, we stand on the edge of destroying the very thing that sustains us, the thing without which this great rational-spiritual dimension of creation itself cannot exist. The irony boggles the mind. What we are destroying is destroying us, body as well as soul. We have made of the earth, just as Francis Bacon insisted in his defense of the new scientific method, "a slave," used it poorly, extracted its labor in our behalf, and killed its spirit.

"Man," Bacon wrote in his justification of the new experimental scientific method, "sinned and fell but he can regain his dominion through science."[10] And sure enough, human—read male—dominance of the earth governs the goal of human enterprise. For centuries now, the position has been a clear one: The earth and all its fruits wait on our needs, or sometimes only our whims, or too often simply on our sins. But they are, in the end, ours. All ours. Interest-

ing, isn't it, that the earth can exist without us but we, superior creatures though we define ourselves to be, cannot exist
without the earth which we are fast destroying, whatever
our intelligence quotients. And all in the name of "taking
dominion."

The Creed gives a testimony to creation that creation
has far too long ignored. God, the Creed insists, created the
earth. The earth, like us, in other words, breathes the breath
of God. The simplicity of the statement overwhelms. What
is it that has been created by God that does not reflect the
presence of God? What is it, created by God, that can cavalierly be destroyed without remorse, without awareness of
the divine life within it? If God is really God, that is. The
Upanishads teach: "As the web issues out of the spider/ And
is withdrawn, as plants sprout from the earth, / As hair grows
from the body, even so, / The sages say, this universe springs
from/ the deathless Self, the source of life."[11]

If anything is the missing link in the spiritual life, the
lost dimension of the Creed, it is disregard for the fate of
the earth and, by extension, therefore, the blatant diminishment of women who become the human counterpart to
"Mother Earth," the supremely fruitful, inherently wild creature whose outpourings we can neither predict nor control.
Women, the savants argued through the ages, were fit for
birthing, for the natural, the carnal, things of life. Men, on the
other hand, obviously unequipped for physical creation, were
made for mental and spiritual creativity. It was a primitive
concept, absorbed by Christianity and legitimated by philosophers and theologians, biologists and judges throughout time—despite the life and teachings of Jesus—to our
very day. Men, men decided, were the lords and masters of
both nature and women, each of whom was a threat to be
overcome. Now the anthropocentric, the human-centeredness
of creation, became the androcentric, the male-centeredness
of life. Males became the center of the universe, the crown

of creation, the norm of the human race. Both women and the earth became invisible to the human soul. Men became the gods of nature, and the God of men became a fiction, kept for Bible-reading but never really applied to life itself.

We have, in other words, set creation at war with itself, all in the name of religion, not only to the detriment of religion but to the desiccation of the spiritual life itself. We have, as a result, left ourselves without a natural path to the Divine. We have also denied ourselves the feminine dimensions and female insights of both life and spirituality, acted as if there aren't any, pretended that one side of the human race was the entire human race and that one experience of God was the only one to be had. Once philosophy made males superior and science made creation inert, and culture made maleness king, the earth lost its meaning to us, the feminine aspect of experience became absorbed, lost, invisible, and that fact that God "created the earth" fell on dulled spirits. We have truncated the spiritual life and come to walk through the fields of creation, the call of the cosmos, deaf, dumb, and blind to its meaning for our souls.

Nature carries great spiritual messages for us all. Nature and its cycles teaches us lessons of balance and harmony, of fidelity and reckless giving. It shows us the glory of the ordinary and dailiness as the ripening part of the godprocess. It gives us an image of sowing and reaping that drives us in good times and sustains us in bad times. It reminds us not to wait for the next world when we should be enjoying this one. Nature soothes our hearts and fills our appetite for freedom and growth, for the sear and the rife. When we are satiated with plastic and gagging on the affectations of a world intent on looking like what it is not, nature calls us back to basics, to beauty, to survival, to becoming.

Then, when we resonate to the natural, we can begin to see within ourselves the clay of natural responses. Then, we can begin to appreciate, to depend on those dimensions of the feminine that have been lost to us in the macho of values limiting to both men and women. We can begin to honor a commitment to compassion, a reverence for feelings, the power of powerlessness, and a connection with life that has been muted, devalued, lost to a world intent on force, "reason," and a manliness that is at best counterfeit. Women are the glue of creation, the bridge between men and earth, totally equal to one and quietly reflective of the godliness of the other. We need the insights of both women and nature in order to redeem and revive the human race.

Instead, we have exalted the value of the human race far beyond any justification for it, become our own gods and so destroyed the sight of the presence of God in the other and the consciousness of our own creaturehood, as well. The Tao reads: "A horse or a cow has four feet. That is Nature. Put a halter around the horse's head and put a string through the cow's nose, that is human. Therefore, it is said, "Do not let humans destroy Nature. Do not let cleverness destroy the natural order."

Today, everywhere in the world, wholistic medicines and therapies and spiritualities are arising to challenge what has become the exaggeration of the rational, the aggrandizement of the scientific, the divinization of the male, the separation of the sexes, the rape of the globe, and the oppression of women. Only the Church lags behind. Only in many of the churches and in the institutions that depend on them for guidance, right-mindedness, and moral values is the discrimination and oppression of women still legitimated in the name of God. Only in the Church does the Creed get short shrift.

Indeed, I believe that God, the fullness of God, is everywhere, in all things, that all things share the same divine life, that they have the same divine end, and that none will come to fullness without the other. Until we stop destroying the globe, we will all starve for something: food, security, peace. Until we stop sexism, men will never grow to full capacity themselves, women will never be seen as the other image of God. Until we stop racism, we will never understand the complexity of God. Until we stop classism, we will never understand that the fullness of creation is meant for all. Until we stop ageism, we will never understand the multiple stages of the processes of nature. Until we stop denying our interconnectedness with the rest of nature we will never find God where God is most clear: in a creation that modern science tells us quite clearly does not pass away, it simply becomes a new kind of energy. To say, "I believe in God...the creator...of earth" is surely a creed to be believed.

I BELIEVE
IN JESUS CHRIST...

I was very young, very intense, very rational and I had just discovered, after ten years in a monastery, that, try as I might, I was no longer sure when I received the Eucharist that the Eucharist could possibly be Jesus. The more I studied, the less I believed in the theology of the Eucharist as I had learned it. I did not really believe that Jesus "was present in the host, body and soul, whole and entire" as the formula I'd learned as a young child stated it. "Don't chew the host," they went so far as to say. "It is the body of Christ. Just swallow it." Unbelievable, I thought now. Soul, maybe, but body? No, I couldn't believe that any more. And if I didn't believe that, did I really believe in Jesus at all? The problem was that I wanted to believe. I wanted to understand it. Otherwise, how could I possibly stay in a monastery any longer?

The young priest to whom I put the question struggled for some basis of explanation. Exasperated after playing an hour of point and counterpoint, he knew when he had an intellectual hard case on his hands. "Do you believe in God?" he said finally. I looked out into the grey sky melting into the grey lake in front of us. I was about to hang my life on this question. I had to believe in something. I eyed the copse of larch behind us and the rolling fields of wildflowers along the horizon. There has to be a source for all of this, I had long ago decided. "Yes," I said slowly and thoughtfully. "I do believe in God. But that's about all I'm sure of," I finished. "Well, then, that's enough," the priest said. "If you believe in God, then you believe that God can do anything and that is enough to know." I closed the conversation quietly. He doesn't know the answer either, I thought as I left the place. But as the years went by, I began to realize that he was, indeed, right. That is the answer. That is enough to know. Whatever words we use to explain the presence of Jesus in my heart may well be wrong. But the presence is powerful.

When I say now, "I believe in Jesus Christ" it is not to the Councils of the Church—to Nicaea or Chalcedon, to Antioch or to Alexandria—to which I turn for confirmation. Those councils represent the problems of another age, of another group of seekers trying to understand who Jesus really is—human or divine or both—and what Jesus really did—save us or atone for us or buy us back from forces in us too deep to name, too fearsome to resist by purely human means. But whatever the answers to those questions, however legitimate they may be, they have little or no interest at all for me. My questions are much deeper than the theological language we use to explain the relationship between God the Creator and Jesus of Nazareth. My questions hearken back to when Jesus himself posed the problem.

After all, Jesus himself asked the disciples two questions. The first, "Whom do others say that I am?" opens up the kind of faith-sharing that brings me into the insights of the rest of humanity about the place of Jesus in the human condition and the divine economy. The struggle of each age to understand again the person and work of Christ, to make a distinction between the Jesus of history and the Christ of faith, to reflect on Jesus as prophet, priest, and king conjure up admirable considerations. No doubt they even identify essential theological considerations, in the face of changing language, changing concepts, changing experiences. But, on the personal level, I have come to be far more interested in the second question that Jesus asks of the disciples, the women, the sick, the lame, the professionals in one form or other, over and over again. "And whom do you say I am?" The first question is the substance of theological seminars, and someone should go on asking it, of course. But the second question is the one meant for me that no one but I can answer. It is the Jesus of my own life and the life of the world around me that I have come to confess in the Creed. It is that Jesus I follow. It is that question that each of us must face sometime in life. And it is that Jesus who captivates me completely.

I believe in the Jesus who fed five thousand simply because they were hungry. Not because they deserved it. Many in the crowd on the hillside in the heat of the day had been foolish, I'm sure: They had brought nothing of their own with them to eat. They had made no provisions for the future. They had not been frugal, not been responsible enough to take care of themselves. But Jesus feeds them regardless. He does not ask to see their salary statements or their bank accounts to determine a degree of acceptable destitution. He does not scold them or berate them or lecture at them. He simply gives them what he sees at that moment that they need.

This is the Jesus whose outpouring of self calls me to do the same. The miracle is not that Jesus multiplied bread and fish, who knows how—by shaming the affluent into sharing their own or by inspiring people to control their greedy appetites or by contravening for an electric moment the laws of nature? The real miracle is that somehow or other the limited resources in that place were shared and came to make do when none of the apostles there believed they would.

I sympathize with those apostles. I look at the poor

waiting in bread lines and part of me, formed in an age of rugged individualism and the notion of unlimited opportunity, wish they would work harder. I am an American, out of a tradition of rugged individualism, and I want them to feed themselves. I am told constantly by the hard-working wealthy, the socially worthy, the politically astute and the working class that there are simply not enough resources to go around. Certainly not enough to give the drones in society, the old people, the children, the sick and the poor plagued by learning disabilities or demons of the mind and heart and soul. I know that I carry that sin within me still. Then, I remember this Jesus and believe in my own need for conversion. Then, I believe in the Jesus Christ who is calling me to work the miracle again.

I believe in the Jesus who raised a young woman from the dead in a culture that taught "When a boy child comes, peace comes. When a girl child comes, nothing comes." Why bother to raise a girl from the dead if her life has no value to begin with? The answer is too obvious to write: Jesus simply does not share the opinion, does not cotton to that philosophy, rejects that theology for the fraud it is. Jesus, born of God, knows that to be made "in the image of God" is not to be shaped male but to be made loving, feeling, thinking. Clearly, to Jesus, this young woman was full of a life force never fully unleashed and meant to come to wholeness yet. But the Jesus who shocked his own culture with his reckless signal that women were human beings, too, was not believed in cultures to come either which, though they came eventually to admit the humanity of women, did not accept their equality. Why bother to educate a girl, society went on saying over and over again. They won't do anything with it. Why bother to ask women what they think about life, about governance, about the world, about even themselves? They don't have sense enough to know. Why bother to beg the Church one more time for inclusive language in theological documents, for two pronouns for the human race, for acknowledgment of the feminine in a genderless God made male by male writers? Why bother— after years and years of patient waiting and endless appeals— to go on knocking on deaf church doors one more time, I tell myself, tired of waiting, weary of closed-minded authoritarianism, and ready to give up and go away to better lands. Why go on for the sake of women until women, too, really become more than partial human beings in a society that is trying and a Church that is not, I ask myself? The answer is clear: We go on because Jesus did. The answer is a matter of faith. The answer is in the Creed. I go on because I believe in the Jesus, the Christ, who raised a woman from the dead.

I believe in the Jesus who cured a cripple on the Sabbath, who said, "Take up your bed and walk"—regardless of the laws regarding Sabbaths. I believe in the Jesus who followed the Law above the law. In a society whose religious ethic made strict demands on pious believers from sundown to sundown of every sabbath, no excuses made, no exceptions given, Jesus required a higher standard. To Jesus, love trumped ritual. The dilemma is obvious: "So the Jews said to the man who had been cured," the Scripture reads, "it is the sabbath; it is not lawful for you to carry your mat." We'll have no moral delinquency here, in other words. No curing people on Sabbaths who had been crippled for years. No carrying of pallets on days of rest. No weighing of one good against another. No departures from tradition. No patience with those who broke the law in the name of the lawgiver. No notion whatsoever that God's ways may not be our ways. No notion that our ideas about the laws of God—about what God really wants—and the laws themselves—what we say God wants—may not, always and everywhere, be the same thing. What, in the face of such a strong religious tradition, is the answer: respect for institutional law and order or recognition of the need for personal love and spiritual development?

I understand the problem. I was not happy as a young woman to see "mixed marriages" that could undermine the denominational attachments, however deep the love, however good might be the families that came from them. I was not pleased to see young people outside my graduate school residence hall marching in the streets, shouting for peace, or crossing national borders to avoid the draft that marked their obligation to the country during the Vietnam War. On the contrary. After all, wasn't national service part of our obedience to God? I myself was getting my degree, keeping the law, being "good." It was a long, hard journey for me from law to conscience. I was not comfortable seeing people leap ahead of the government and refuse the use of force, leap ahead of liturgical rubrics to take Communion in the hand, now so seemingly small a thing, then so major a blurring of the lay and the clerical role. It was troubling to hear about people, priests, nuns, parishes ignoring the rules here, bending the rules there, whatever the agony over birth control pills and celibacy and religious life and the needs of women. We needed to be patient. We needed to obey. We needed to "work things through." What would the Church say? What did the law require? What did citizenship demand?

The questions were real ones. The answer, I came to understand, was the Jesus who said, "Take up your mat and walk." Sometimes the law inflicts more suffering for the sake of its own preservation than it preserves the climate that makes the Gospel possible. I believe in the Jesus who looked at a person who had been crippled, misjudged, and oppressed for thirty-eight years, ignored on the hillside of the Healing Pool for thirty-eight years, called to fullness of life and denied it for thirty-eight years—all in the name of the Law—and, Sabbath or no Sabbath, cured him. In that moment, law did not become lawlessness. In that moment, love gave law a new criterion.

Truly this one is of God. Through the humanity of Jesus shines the Divine. In Jesus, the Way becomes both clear and possible, plain and imperative. We see in Jesus the mind of God. We also see that this great presence was a human presence. It is, therefore, a presence possible to us as well. More than that, it is a presence expected of us. Therein lies the difficulty.

It is not so much the theological formulations that underlie the Creed that the Creed professes. The Creed simply lays claim to the Jesus of lepers and women, the poor and the pleading, the sick and the sinful, and in so doing calls us to acknowledge the benchmark of our own lives. The Creed reminds us of the Jesus who laying hands on the needy, lays hands on us and requires us to do the same to the black brother, the overlooked woman, the irresponsible poor who come seeking bread and inclusion and resurrection of the spirit.

Jesus is the Way. Who is there who does not want to know the way before the journey begins? Who does not seek to know the end toward which they press? Who does not attempt to measure themselves against what they are trying to become? Jesus is God's measure, end, and scheme for all of us, all laws aside, all tradition to the contrary.

Jesus, the Creed calls us to realize, stands before us, the clearest, sharpest, most fulsome picture we have of the face of God. And how can we be sure of that? Because Jesus is what we know in our hearts God must surely be: compassionate, just, merciful, loving, and on the other side of every boundary. It is Jesus with the Samaritan Woman, Jesus with the little children, Jesus with the prisoner, Jesus immersed in God that I must become if the Creator-God is ever to see divinity come to fullness of life in me, as well.

The Creed calls me far beyond the formulations of

Nicaea, Constantinople, and Chalcedon, beyond legalisms and political pettiness, beyond precision with words to depth of understanding, beyond conformity to conscience, to recognition of my connection with all of creation. When I say, "I believe in Jesus" I am saying that I believe in a way of life above and beyond what anything else challenges me to be. Institutions, the best of them, want me in the end for the aggrandizement, the status, the power, the service of themselves. They want me to keep their rules and regulations, their laws and disciplines, their priorities and prescriptions, all of them, without a doubt, good. But all of them partial. Short of the goal. Only Jesus wants me for more than that. Jesus wants me for the Gospel, for the Good Life, whatever the cost. That is the Jesus in whom I believe.

9

GOD'S ONLY SON.

Why didn't you and daddy ever have any more children?" I asked my mother. I was about four years old. "If God had wanted to send us more children, we would have been very happy to have them," my mother said. "But once we saw you, we knew we had everything we could ever want in the whole world and we didn't need anything else." I left the room floating about four inches off the floor. I was everything my parents ever wanted. The incident affected my life for years. And, without my realizing it, it touched my prayer life, too. I know what it meant to be "an only son."

When I look back now, I realize that the very fact that I was an only child made it perfectly sensible to me to say a Creed that pointed out that Jesus was "the only Son of God." I had no problem accepting the implications of that statement at all. At least not until I got older. I knew better than anybody else in my class, in fact, what the phrase was meant to say. The others all had brothers and sisters to whom to talk, with whom to play, from whom to learn, with whom to compete for attention. But when you are an "only" child, I knew, you are the center of the universe, the one carrier of all the hope in the family, the one mirror of a parent's life, the only complete picture of themselves that a parent has. At the same time, not only do you get all of their attention but you give your parents all of yours, as well. The only child lives in an adult world and takes on adult interests and adult concerns and adult lifestyles and adult perspectives. Nothing distracts the only child from becoming the carbon copy of the one model before them, the adult one, the parental one, the one for whom life has already waxed well and whole. The only child becomes both parents: the father's "son" as well as his little girl; the "mother's little helper" as well as her daughter. In its "onlyness" alone, lies its specialness. To call Jesus "the only Son of God," then, is an image that carries great weight. It carries meanings far beyond the obvious one. It is a powerful statement. But it is also an unfortunate one—and now sometimes even a divisive one. There are problems with the title that no amount of historical explanation can completely erase. It rankles. It also raises serious theological questions in an age coming out of patriarchy into the bright, clear light of universalism.

"Sonship," the very sociological term itself, is an expression that brings with it clear overtones of exclusion. There is no such thing in the English language, for instance, as "daughtership." "Daughtership" is not a role. It carries no weight, has no meaning, implies no power, embodies no hope—either for the parent or for the daughter herself. Sons are people with defined family responsibility or identity or mantle; daughters simply come with the family, faceless, anonymous and engulfed in shadow. Sons rise to inherited positions and power and identity. Daughters fade into the fog of family history. To talk about Jesus as the "only Son of God," then, says something to women that it does not say to men simply by what it fails to say to women at all. But it also has said something to men that has deformed them. God does not have daughters. God has sons.

That's when I began to falter on this phrase of the Creed. What was really meant here? That Jesus and everybody like him, meaning men, could have an intense, intimate, personal, authentic, identifying relationship with God but that

I and my kind could not? How could I say I believed something like that when in my heart I knew it was not true? In my soul it was not real. God resonated there as clearly as in the soul of any man. God resided in me as certainly as God resided in the soul of anyone else I'd ever seen. God and I were in intimate dialogue. And Jesus was the glue of it, the reflection of it, the Way of it. I knew its power and I could not surrender it to a biology, a philosophy that named half of what God created lesser than the other half of what God had created. I, too, had inherited the presence of God in my soul, my heart, my life. I knew the passion for the Divine in myself. Creed or no Creed, how could I possibly say that I believed in a sexist God, a God who chose sons but not daughters?

But "Jesus was male," after all. So what else is there to say? And how can women be offended by it? What is there not to believe about the statement that "Jesus is the only Son of God?" The answer depends, I began to realize, on what you really intend the statement to say. It all depends on what the faith really demands that we mean when we say it. The concept is not as simple as it may seem at face value.

The phrase "God's only son" has a tortured history, more ecclesiastically political than simply theological and always more interpretive than illustrative. To the early church, the Church of the councils that designated it, it was meant more to distinguish Christianity from other current religious understandings and Jesus from other lesser religious figures than it was to describe a patriarchal God. The phrase meant to answer the heretics of the day, the Gnostics, who argued that out of the Supreme Deity emanated multiple demiurges or lesser deities. These, they argued, were responsible for Creation. The Creed, on the other hand, asserted that God was One, and that the relationship between God and Jesus was unique, one and only, none other like it anywhere. Jesus was not a demiurge or a lesser deity. Jesus was of God. The difference between that idea and the notion that God chose sons over daughters challenges all the unsaid arguments that make "After all, Jesus was male," an argument for exclusion.

The phrase also meant to signal to a non-Christian world—long accustomed to using the same phrase, "Son of God," to assert for their King a claim to divine origin—that here was a relationship eminently more kingly but vastly different than the kings of the world. This God was not a potentate and this Jesus had no desire to be anything so paltry as a bureaucratic king. This God was not one among many and this Jesus was not a politician pretending to be divine, this Jesus was not just anybody. On the contrary. This was a relationship unlike any relationship the world had ever known. The cosmic God had brought forth Godness itself in human embryo. A startling thought and a liberating one. If humanity itself had birthed godness, then all of humanity could, potentially, aspire to an intimate relationship with God.

The purpose of the phrase, interestingly enough, has never been to make the point that Jesus is a man or that the genderless God is male. It attempts simply to say in words that falter what is as unthinkable perhaps as it is unsayable. It says that within the human condition there is the stuff, the energy, the magnetism, the basis for a relationship with God. And we know it because we have seen it in the relationship of Jesus, our kind, to the God, beyond us, from whom He springs. The problem is that in the attempt to build us all in this very phrase, in the hands of the narrow-minded or unaware, manages to build half of us out. "God the Father" and "God the Son," however benignly meant, have been distorting images.

The implications are astounding: Jesus is the unique child of God, with everything that implies, with all that means for us who strive to become like Jesus. Each of us has the right to a unique relationship with the God in whose womb we are carried. Each of us bears in our own souls the mirror of God. Each of us breathes divine life within us. Each of us is everything God loves uniquely.

When I pray the Creed, then, I hold in my heart the hope of a relationship with God that is my own and which I trust I can achieve because, like Jesus, I was made for it. Pray to God as "Abba," Jesus tells us, adding another theological dimension—God as parent—to the then common understanding of God as God the Creator, God the Judge. In the earliest liturgies of the Church, for instance, the first written record of a eucharistic service written in the early third century, Jesus is not called the only "son" of God. Jesus is called "the child of God." Twice.[12] The purpose of the Creed, in other words, is not to paint a biology of God or of Jesus. The Creed sets out to assert a unique bond. Jesus and God are intimates and Jesus, the human one, stands as our invitation, our proof, that we can be the same. Call God, "Abba," Jesus tells us all. Play the child, in other words, on the lap of your creator. You will be nursed and nurtured, rocked and raised to wholeness. You will be filled with everything you need. The point is not that you will not be denied. The point is that you will be denied nothing you honestly, seriously, actually need to bear the unbearable and be better for it.

We, too, are each a unique child of God. Jesus' humanity is our proof of it. Our creator did not create humanity and fling it into empty, endless space unaware of it, and, worse, uncaring of it. Your God, like your own parents, created you, initiated you, evolved you, provided for you what you need and watches breathless for your well-being as you use it.

In this phrase lies the divine dimension of a Creed written to call humanity to fullness. It provides a paragon of what I myself can be. It promises the fulfillment of what now I can only hope for in the basest part of me—that I, too, was made for glory, that I too can grow into the truest

part of me, that even I can become what I was made to be
out of the substance of divinity.

When I pray, "I believe in Jesus Christ, the only child of
God," I am saying that I believe in the fullness of what I
myself can become. I cannot be male, however. If that is
what is required of this relationship, if it is biological and
not spiritual, then not only can I not have it, I don't want it.
Such a God is not a God of women. But then, you see, the
thing that's wrong with ascribing sex to God is that such a
God would not be God at all. And we would never become
fully human enough, any of us, to become what we must.
"Where is God?" someone wrote on a barracks wall in
Auschwitz. But beneath it, legend tells us, someone else wrote
the more impelling answer: "Where are human beings?"
We did not need God to save the Jews from the Holocaust.
We needed God alive in us. The problem is that God comes
alive in us only after we learned to live in God. Jesus, the
human who proves that divinity is our calling, is the sign of
our call to do that, our ability to do that. But if doing it
depends on being an "only son," rather than a child of God,
then not only are women disparaged but so also is God.

When I say, "I believe in Jesus Christ, the unique, the
only child of God," I am praying to become the relationship I seek in my own heart. And it is the Jesus born of a
woman by a genderless God who is my proof that such a
bond is not open to sonship only.

I believe. The only difference is that I believe more what
they mean than what they say.

10

OUR LORD...

L ife," Kierkegaard wrote, "can only be understood backwards; but it must be lived forwards."[13] Perspective is a powerful tool. It can also be a deceptive one. Once we come to understand a thing, we often fail to see it as it really is, as it was when first we experienced it. Once understanding comes, we seldom see a thing the same way again. We read back into it what has, over time, become clear but which we did not recognize at the beginning. We begin to be enamored of it in ways that had no meaning at its outset. On the day we begin to love someone, for instance, we find ourselves seeing them differently than we did the day before. We suddenly see all there is to see of them now, all at once. We forget how they looked to us at the beginning of the relationship. We can even forget what it was about them that first attracted us so much. The little things that charmed us blur and fade and merge with the larger picture. Their natural abilities suddenly become talents, their intelligence becomes brilliance, what we once called their social poise we now call magnetism. What we once took at face value we now expound and embellish, explain and analyze and, often, enlarge. We do it with everything, not just with people. We have a real capacity for turning the simple into the abstruse.

When we learn some subject well, we regard its intricacies with more respect. We get a new taste for its complexi-

ties. We recognize its many degrees of proficiency. When we
unmask new meaning in the moment, we remember it with
a special gleam and at the same time forget that there was a
time when we did not see what we could not see. Familiar-
ity doesn't breed contempt. It breeds the kind of concentrated focus that too often fixes on one dimension of a thing
to the exclusion of all its other facets. To say, "I believe in
Jesus Christ...our Lord" does the same. It focuses on a single
penetrating, revealing, defining aspect of the Christ and may,
as a result, obscure a bit the consciousness of how this lordship actually functioned in Jesus. And with serious consequences for us all. The images we cherish of Jesus become
the patterns upon which we build the Church, our institutions, the values of our own lives. "Lord" has certainly been
one of those. Only after the Resurrection did the early
Church call Jesus "Lord," meaning the "divine one," the
one equal to God, rather than "Lord" meaning "master."[14]
Before that, as Jesus walked the earth, talked to people, at-
tended the synagogue, went to dinner parties, preached on
hillsides, hung on the cross, Jesus had been teacher, master,
rabbi, prophet, son of David, King of the Jews—all titles
the Jewish people knew well. "Lord," the community's understanding of Jesus that came with Easter, in the end, may
have, over the long haul, obscured as much as it revealed.
Jesus, the "Lord," this Jesus who embodied sacred power,
this Jesus whose triumph over death revealed his Godhead,
was Divine Lord, King of land and sea, earth and heaven,
matter and spirit, of all "that was and is to be." To him,
Paul wrote, "every knee shall bend and every head shall
bow." The transition was a mighty one. Forgotten now, or
only barely remembered at best, was the Jesus who spent
days tramping the dirty roads of Galilee. Gone the memories of a Jesus bent and bleeding and bound before the throne
of Pilate. Completely overlooked now was the Jesus whom
his family called crazy and the synagogue called an imposter

and the state called a rabble-rouser. "Understanding" had set in and with it amnesia for the kind of lord the Lord had really been.

I never understood the problem more clearly than I did standing for the first time in St. Peter's Basilica in Rome. Everybody else, tourists from everywhere in the world, were looking up at the grand frescoes and larger-than-life marble statues of popes no one had even heard of, let alone remembered. I, on the other hand, found myself returning again and again to something on the floor. Every so many feet, it seemed, there were words inlaid in the marble. I stretched around the feet of tour groups to read them. For a while, the inscriptions had no meaning to me at all. I simply could not understand why the names of all the other major basilicas in the world had been imbedded in the floor of this one. Then, little by little, the murkiness of the message began to clear. Every name of every cathedral inset in the floor was followed by a number: the length of its nave. The implication was obvious now: If you brought the Basilica of St. John Lateran and put it down in here, it would only fill this much of this basilica. If you brought the Hagia Sophia here, it would only fill this much more of this basilica. If you brought....Suddenly, the light dawned: I was standing in the middle of one of the most blatant games of ecclesiastical one-upmanship I had ever seen. This was "Jesus, our Lord" with a vengeance. This was medieval pomp and circumstance enough to give Versailles comeuppance. This is what happens when we forget what made the Lord lord, and how the Lord was lord.

And who has not seen it? Arbitrary power used arbitrarily in the name of Jesus has far too often been called "obedience," when obedience to whom and why and for what was either most uncertain, or too certain entirely. Someone with no right whatsoever to compel another uses "obedience" to demand what they are not entitled to demand by nature. Ecclesiastical bureaucrats overstep their bounds and call those who protest lacking in faith. Or, more likely, someone who has every legal right to command obedience commands it imperiously, to the degradation of the persons on whom they impose it. And they do it in the name of the Lord, in the interest of salvation, for the sake of truth and honor and goodness. They make a travesty of authority and call it "divine."

But underneath the curdling of divine power into human power, another Lord remains, a constant comment on an authoritarianism passing for authority, a clear criterion of human lordship wherever it rages: in you and me when we evaluate the staff without consideration for differences, in the local pastor when he fires the liturgist for using inclusive language in the hymns, in the bishop when he refuses Communion to people who belong to targeted groups, in the Vatican when it suppresses theologians who ask for dialogue on difficult issues, in the pope when he tells the world what they may and may not think about sacramentally under pain of excommunication. Indeed, lordship, leadership, authority are complex issues in a modern world. But they are not synonyms. When we talk about Jesus as Lord, we find ourselves holding in tension two incompatible concepts: imperial power and a bleeding Jesus whose crucifixion comes without hosts of angels and whose Resurrection comes silently. The Creed brings us to review them both again and again and again.

In a computerized world, where power and authority become more and more invisible, more and more controlling, more and more universal every day, the concepts may be crucial ones. Privacy is gone. The safety of distance is gone. Dialogue is gone in the most democratic societies the world has ever known. Talk is plenty, but dialogue, the communication of equals seeking a common solution to a common question, is gone in a system where more and more centralization everywhere camouflages authoritarianism anywhere. Power rests at the top and the top cannot be found or, if found, cannot be approached and, if approached, cannot be contacted. It is a world of electronic answering machines, penthouse suites, stock proxies, and disbanded committees.

In a globalized world, authority becomes more and more ruthless every day. In a nuclearized world, authority becomes more and more dangerous every day. Without a spirituality of authority, the modern world teeters on the brink of power gone wild, the church no less than the state. The long arm of authority, stronger than ever before in history, reaches into the tiniest recesses of contemporary society. George Orwell's "Big Brother" lives in the twenty-first century, alive, well, and growing stronger by the day. Orders are instant now. Supervision is immediate. Cameras and computerized reports are the order of the day. Accountability is required on a massive scale. And all of that is wonderful beyond comprehension if the theory of authority upon which it rests is healthy, is sane.

At its inception, "authority" meant "to promote" and "to enrich." Now, it means "to control or to govern." The thoughts are sobering. They are also enlightening. Jesus governed no one. Jesus enriched everyone. And the people said, "He spoke as one who had 'authority.'"

The personal authority of Jesus far outweighed the official authority of the systems around him. He wore no phylacteries. He rode on donkeys. He held no positions. And he listened to everyone. He listened to blind beggars and foreign soldiers and small children and contentious Pharisees and hemorrhaging women. His only rules were love. He went about forgiving sins and curing ills and confronting the legalisms of the institution so that people could be free. He preached that when mercy and peace and compassion and justice set into a people, that the kingdom of God

broke into their lives at the same time. And they followed
him from one end of the country to the other in droves. He
was the Lord without lordliness. No chains, no miters, no
thrones, no public relations advisors. He lorded it over no
one. He died on a cross and compelled an empire.

The One the Creed calls Lord is the image of a powerful
God who does not impose even good. This God lives to be
poured out in creation and uses no force to have it accepted.
This God's sun shines, the psalmist noted, "on both the just
and the unjust." It excludes no one, bathes the whole world,
believer and nonbeliever alike, with the fruits of the earth,
the joy of life, the goodness of creation. This Lord is the
presence of God among the people, not the presence of force
or pomp or prestige among the powerless.

But the memory of that kind of authority is dimmed by
the trappings of power, the oppression of the powerful, the
favoring of institutional control over the needs of the women
today who ask to be cured of their stoopedness and the
hungry who seek food now on the Sabbath. I find myself no
longer impressed by a church that bases its authority on
only slightly veiled references to "bell, book, and candle,"
the excommunication process that pronounces those who
question the givens of the day dead in spirit, dead in soul,
dead to the Church, and no longer loyal to governments
that get their way at the long end of a Cruise missile.

My Creed pays homage only to the Lord who gazed
patiently on the rich young man whose commitment was
yet only partial, who refused to punish prostitutes, who
broke no bruised reeds, and who counseled Peter to "forgive the other seven times seventy times." It is the model for
my own use of authority, however much I fail at it. It is the
authority, the lordship, for which I seek, however often it
escapes me. Tom Gumbleton, the auxiliary bishop of Detroit, in Haiti; Samuel Ruiz Garcia, the bishop of Chiapas,
Mexico, sitting with Indians in a lean-to in a Zapatista camp

in Chiapas, Mexico; Daniel Berrigan, a Jesuit priest, doing time in a Massachusetts jail for civil disobedience; Dorothy Day, laywoman and prophet, protesting war; Mother Jones, immigrant Irish laborer, inciting labor protests; John Paul II forgiving his assassin; the women of "Womanchurch," creating havens of liturgical inclusiveness for women—these are all forms of authority I understand, I believe in, I want myself to be. But the system, however sincere, that sets out to outbuild the basilicas before it, to silence women, to suppress thought, to force compliance with things that need to be questioned, I do not.

When I pray, "I believe in Jesus Christ...our Lord" I do not ever mean to imply that I believe in anything less than that, in anything which only masquerades as lord by playing at lordship. The Creed calls us to remember the Jesus we knew before the Resurrection so that following him thereafter we might use human authority to imitate his outpouring of love, instead of trying ourselves to assume his glory before our time.

HE WAS
CONCEIVED BY
THE HOLY SPIRIT...

I t happened the year I was in England. I had returned to
Cambridge for the Michaelmas term to complete the
work I was doing there as Research Fellow of the Von
Hugel Institute. But, as much as I wanted to be at Cambridge, it was not turning out to be an easy period for me.
In early July of that year, I had broken both feet and spent
four months in casts, crutches, and now a cane. It was beginning to look as if the pain would be chronic and my
movements limited for a long time, if not permanently—no
simple situation in what Europeans euphemistically call "a
walking city." I was adjusting to both ideas relatively well,
considering the speed at which I'm accustomed to moving
and the circumstances I was in. In fact, the only acceptable
approach to the situation, now that the physical therapy
routine had done all it seemed able to do, seemed to be the
philosophical one: What is, is after all.

In late October of that term, still using the cane, I gave
a public workshop at another college in the city, a seminar
on the place of women in the Church and society. In the
final segment of the morning presentation, I talked about
the power of God working through women in Scripture. At

the end of the session, a white-haired woman, still speaking with a thick French accent after years in an English culture, came up to the podium to tell me that she knew without doubt that the power of God worked through her. "See these hands?" she said, spreading them out palms down in front of me to emphasize the point. "There is the power of God in these hands." She was, she went on to explain, a healer. Unlike doctors who treat people medically, she was clearly telling me, she prayed over sick people and they got well. "I could have used you four months ago," I said lightly, bantering really, making small talk at best, but certainly not seriously interested in the process for myself. My prayer patterns, formed for years in a monastic setting, lean toward far more traditional styles. She gave me a long, lean look. I was sitting by this time, waiting for the lecture hall to empty so I could leave the room without the limp being noticed. I was in no mood to tell the whole story again.

When the afternoon session ended, suddenly she was back again. "I will do a healing for you," she kept insisting. "No, no," I said as politely but as firmly as I could. "Thank you very much for your concern, but my cab is waiting." All I wanted to do was to get out of that hall and off my feet. She followed me to the front of the college and, seeing that the cab was not really there yet, dropped to one knee in front of me on the street. *Oh, no, you don't*, I thought with a rush of embarrassment and reached down to pull her up. But before I could do anything to stop her, I felt a piercing heat go through the breakpoint in my foot. Then, she got up out of her kneeling position, saying to herself as she did, "Thanks be to God for whatever gift has been given" and walked into the crowds on Jesus Street. I have never had a pain in that foot since. And I have never said this phrase of the Creed quite the same again, either.

The situation is plain: The Creed does not tell me *how* Jesus was conceived by the Holy Spirit. The Creed simply tells me *that* Jesus was conceived by the Holy Spirit. I am being asked to believe, in other words, that Jesus was born under the impulse of the Spirit of the Holy. Never mind how. The manner of that conception is undefined; perhaps, I have come to think as my faith matured, even unimportant. In some ways, it is far more difficult to believe that God acts through normal channels than it is to believe that God acts through unnatural ones. From another perspective, what is so unusual about the unusual? That this conception was incomparable, different, beyond common expectations, under the marked impulse of God, is clear. But then, so was the birth of Isaac, the son of Abraham and Sarah who were promised a child long after the natural order of things would suggest the possibility of such an event. So, too, was the birth of John the Baptist, whose mother, Elizabeth, Scripture tells us, was also barren. So, in fact, are a lot of things unusual, different, beyond normal expectations. People with gifts of healing, for instance, are unusual. People who play music they cannot read, for instance, are different. People with extrasensory perception, who read messages in sealed envelopes, go far beyond normal expectations. Who can explain any of them "scientifically"? Who knows how it happens? But who has not seen the effect of the Spirit in the natural world around them.

When I realized how unusual life usually is, I began to read this segment of the Creed differently. I began to understand that the purpose of this thesis is not to explain the process of conception. It makes no attempt to explain anything technical. The purpose of this statement is to make a point far more important than science. It is not a negative commentary on the baseness of human sexuality. On the contrary. It is a declaration of the inherent divine impulse fundamental to the birth of Jesus, proper to humanity, and available to us all. It is a testimony to the power of the Spirit working through the commonplace of humanity. And it is that in which I believe. I believe that Jesus is the Holy One of God, the outpouring of the Holy Spirit, the presence of God in our midst. I believe that in the humanity of Jesus lies the glory of us all. The thought is awesome in its implications for lives lost in the humdrum, weighed down by depression, dulled to the divinity around them, and discouraged by their own limitations.

If Jesus is the Breath of the Spirit, if the Spirit can work through the humanity of Jesus, then the Spirit can work through our humanity, as well. Humanity is not inimical to holiness. The flesh is not evil. Then, the connection between flesh and spirit makes miracles of us all.

It is a glorious statement of faith, this notion that the Divine does not reject the human. It stands as highpoint of the Christian tradition, challenging centuries of dualism, even in Christianity itself. But the point is not easily made. Not then, not now. For those in the early Church who saw Jesus only as divine, the flesh became a burden, an obstacle to spiritual development, the pitfall, the trap of being human. If Jesus was only a kind of ethereal copy of the human, as proponents of the spiritual nature of Jesus argued, then humanity was just as bereft without Jesus as with him. If, on the other hand, the Spirit actually worked through the humanity of Jesus, as the early councils argued back, then humanity was the stuff of divine action in all of us.

At the same time, for those who saw Jesus only as human, then the human quest for accessibility to the divine had nowhere to look for hope. If in him there was no bridge to God, then where were they to look?

The two positions struggled for ascendancy. As a result, the recognition of the Spirit in the human condition suffers a tenuous history. The Creed proclaims that belief in Jesus, "conceived by the Holy Spirit," in the Spirit of the Holy, offers eternal promise because the Jesus of Nazareth is also the Christ of Faith. Jesus, one in whom both humanity and

divinity are whole, shows a Way, renews hope in the midst
of confusion, makes of despair short shrift. Jesus, the Creed
promises us, gives us God's guide to Godness, gives us divinity of soul in the heart of humanity.

Probably no other single religious issue has plagued
humanity, shaped culture, or affected personal development
more than the way religion looks at the question of the flesh.
The notion that spirit and flesh were of a piece, that the
breath of God breathed in us all, a concept deeply rooted in
the Jewish tradition, was denied by Greek philosophy, abandoned by Gnostic Christians in the early Church, and subject to all manner of assault ever since. From Manicheanism
to the Penitential Movement, from Puritanism to French
and Irish Jansenisms, the social pendulum has swung, even
in our own time, from repudiation of nature to almost complete abandonment to it as life's only value. Religious zeal-
ots have denied the rights of the flesh, whipped the flesh,
starved the flesh, and cursed the flesh. Religious libertines
have abandoned themselves to the demands of the flesh to
the point of sopping, self-destructive physical excesses in
celebration of "freedom." Where is the sanity, where is the
sanctity, between those two extremes?

The Creed is clear: Matter and spirit are of a piece. To
those who ask whether flesh is the burden of humanity or its
blessing, the conception of Jesus makes the answer explicit. If
the presence of God can be contained in the flesh, then all
flesh holds the holy in its grasp, all flesh is under the impulse
of God. The realization is awesome. The flesh that weakens
under every conceivable pressure, is, at the same time, the
flesh that sustains the human quest for holiness, nourishes
it, maintains it through hard times, and enables it always.

The flesh that human beings in their ardor for perfection disdain as dangerous, God has filled with an insatiable
capacity for the divine. In fact, without a healthy awareness
of both the potential and the problems of the flesh, no

amount of perfection can ever come to the wholeness for which we were made. We learn as we get older how easy it is to be perfect and to be steeped in sin at the same time. We hold ourselves to rules and judge the lawless and never realize how sinful the law can be. Jesus knew that it was a sin to keep people hungry and crippled on the Sabbath. We know, down deep, that ostracizing gays and abandoning AIDS patients and executing criminals is wrong, but, hidden behind law, it can all look so holy, so righteous. Life is complex and sin is often the way to God, hard as it is to admit it. Indeed, perfection is at once a goal and a ruse.

What good is a perfection that has never known failure? Perfection is only the ability to achieve beyond our imperfections. The truth is that one needs the other to exist. People are not born perfect; they become perfect by failing. And, interestingly enough, we call it practice in every arena but the spiritual. There we call it failure. What a pity. By squeezing the deficiencies out of ourselves without exploring them, their meanings, their invitations to grow in ways we never expected, we lose the depth of the quest. We miss the process of the journey with all its paroxysms, all its learnings, all its possibilities. We lose the practice of the soul. What good is it to punish the body to the point that we can think of nothing else and call that kind of self-destruction the pursuit of perfection? What does that practice achieve, except personal obliteration at the level of the soul? It is only when we practice humanity at its best that we find the soul is us that life is meant to develop.

We practice finding beauty by learning to recognize the base. We practice endurance by learning the uselessness, the deprivation, the lack of it. And we learn the spiritual life for which we are destined by stretching humanity to the fullness of its divine potential, by remembering that Jesus was conceived by the Holy Spirit, by taking hope from the Spirit of Holiness in ourselves.

The Jesus who was "conceived by the Holy Spirit" not only reminds us of the Spirit within but shows us the character of the life we shape by opening ourselves to the impulse of a God who, daily, leads us beyond ourselves. As Jesus responded to the Spirit in his own life, so we realize can we. As Jesus was formed by it, so we now know are we. The awareness of the Spirit within us is the awareness of the Cosmic, created by God and embodied in Jesus.

The Spirit opened Jesus to a world beyond his own. The Spirit does the same for us, if only we allow ourselves to become bigger than the limitations of a humanity in which the divinity has never been unleashed. We tie ourselves to the religions of the world: to national chauvinism, to religious intolerance, to racist conclusions and sexist structures and call it fidelity to the law of God. But all the while, the conception of Jesus leads us to reach out to the Samaritan Woman, the Roman soldier, the needy in our midst where the Holy Spirit is also working, also struggling to bring life to the full.

The conception, the impulsion, the kindling of Jesus by the Spirit of the Holy calls us to become less concentrated on sin and more on grace, less concerned with the restrictions of law and more with the limitless possibilities of love, less obsessed by the limitations of being human and more in awe of its potential. It is humanity that is the womb of the divine for us. That I believe.

12

AND BORN...

I remember standing in the crypt of the small church in Bethlehem. We had been driven in an Arab bus by Arab guides through the shuttered Arab towns that lay between Jerusalem and Bethlehem to one of the central shrines of the Christian world, the place where Jesus, the stories told, had been born. Now the streets were empty, the shops closed, the window displays covered with metal blinds. Roadblocks were set up at strategic points along the road to check Arab cars, Arab trucks that plied their way back and forth along the route between work in the Jewish city and home in the Arab villages. Arab children popped out of doorways or peeked around street corners to watch us go by. The city had been empty of tourists for days. In the public square, Jewish soldiers sat in jeeps mounted with machine guns. There was passion on both sides and sullen determination everywhere. These were foreigners in their own land, both the Arabs and the Jews. The Arabs had been there forever and were now displaced. The Jews, after hundreds of years, finally had themselves a country in which they were not welcome. Every muscle in my body was tight. This place could explode at any moment.

I looked across the hillsides that surrounded the village and the church. I tried to imagine David and his sheep, a young man and his pregnant wife, a band of angels and a human birth. Of all of them, it was the thought of the human birth that stirred me most. The angels and the stable, the donkey and the sheep, the census and the inn I did not care about. What affected me deeply, however, was the thought of the birth. Somewhere, somehow Jesus of Nazareth had been born here, in the same kind of environment that existed here today—into a culture where people were strangers in their own lands and soldiers walked the streets to control them. It was a political insight. It was a deeply, disturbingly human one. If Jesus was born into this, and brought the presence of God into its midst and changed attitudes in the heart of it, then so could we. So must we.

The candle that hangs over an embedded marble star illuminates a point on the earth where, tradition says, God took the initiative to make humanity more human. We remember it always with lights and tinsel, with bells and incense, with parties and ornaments. We forget the political impact of it, the psychological demands of it, the spiritual implications of it. We live unconscious of the fact to which the Creed can call us back, over and over again: Christmas is a movable feast, a feast that changes in meaning as we move through life growing more and more aware of its real significance for us. We were born. Jesus was born. What Jesus did to survive life, to bear life, to create life, to become life, we can do as well. Or better: What we do to survive life, to bear life, to create life, to become life, Jesus did before us. Our struggles are not new. Our questions are not senseless. Our burdens are not unbearable.

Christmas, the remembrance of the birth of Jesus, is not a remembrance at all. It is an awareness that grows in us from day to day all our lives. Christmas, this consciousness of eternal Life alive among us, is not a feast day, it is a ferial day that never ends. It is a call to make today better than yesterday because on a day just like today, Christ did it before us.

Christmas is a strange season. When you're a child, it is a season of presents. When you're young, it's a season of parties. When you get your own home, it's a season of preparations. But when you get older, Christmas changes color drastically. Suddenly, out from behind the advertisements and big dinners, through the haze of old carols and soft candles, past the dazzling altars and sumptuous crib scenes, we begin to see what Christmas is really all about. Christmas is about finding life where we do not expect life to be.

Every year of life waxes and wanes. Every stage of life comes and goes. Every facet of life is born and then dies. Every good moment is doomed to become only a memory. Every perfect period of living slips through our fingers and disappears. Every hope dims and every possibility turns eventually to dry clay. Until Christmas comes again. Then we are called at the deepest, most subconscious, least cognizant level to begin once more to live newly again.

Christmas brings us all back to the crib of life to start over: aware of what has gone before, conscious that nothing can last, but full of hope that this time, finally, we can learn what it takes to live well, grow to full stature of soul and spirit, get it right.

There is a child in each of us waiting to be born again. It is to those looking for life that the figure of the Christ, a child, beckons. Christmas is not for children. It is for those who refuse to give up and grow old, for those to whom life comes newly and with purpose each and every day, for those who can let yesterday go so that life can be full of new possibility always, for those who are agitated with newness whatever their age. Life is for the living, for those in whom Christmas is a feast without finish, a celebration of the constancy of change, a call to begin once more the journey to human joy and holy meaning.

Let the soldiers stomp through life. Let the cold winds blow. Let the birth points of all our lives be drowned in obscurity. Let the days seem mundane and fruitless. This place in Bethlehem, cold, dark, small, worn down by years of discovery, justifies them all. Jesus has been here before us. Bring on the days of our lives. We have a God who has already walked them and found them holy-making.

We knelt down on the marble floor, the sticky August day steaming around us, and we sang "O Little Town of Bethlehem" slowly and softly. "The hopes and fears of all the years," we sang with new conviction, new understanding, "are met in thee tonight." The fact that it was August, not December, made December more meaningful than ever and August more demanding than ever.

Up on the street, an old Arab man was selling a Christmas crèche made from rough-carved olive wood old enough to have been there the night that Christ was born. He had not seen a tourist to whom he could sell his wares for weeks, and his eyes were pleading. I bought the set and boarded the bus. Surely that is what Christmas is really about. Surely every day is meant to be Christmas. Surely every day Christ is trying to be born in us again.

The Arabs drove us back through the Jewish checkpoints, past the same machine guns as before, beyond the villages where Arab uprisings were constant. But life looked different now. I wasn't afraid anymore. Jesus had been born into the very world in which I myself was living. And weathered it and loved it and changed it. Whatever the difficulty of any other dimension of belief, this element was obvious. No historian had ever doubted it or contested it or challenged the truth of it. Jesus had been born. The synagogue took issue with him. The state feared him. The people saw in him a figure like no other. Clearly, the face of God had shone upon us. What else could I possibly need to live my own life more fully?

OF THE
VIRGIN MARY...

Folklore is replete with delightful stories about the understanding of Mary and Mariology in the daily life of the Church. One story tells of an old man, intent on receiving a special favor, who prayed fervently every day at the shrine of Mary, the Mother of God. Impressed by such devotion, Jesus himself, the story continues, decided to reward such faith by appearing in person to assure the man of the blessings that would come to him. Seeing the Christ Child standing above the altar where he was accustomed to seeing the statue of Mary, the old man, intent on his prayers and irritated by the interruption, barked, "Go away, little boy. I wanna talk to your momma."

Of all the segments of the Creed that touch the lives of people, the integrity of the Church, and the nature of society yet today, "born of the Virgin Mary" may surely be it. Behind this simple statement lie allusions that have frozen society into interpretations of Scripture, models of Church, and notions of sexuality that affect it to this day. Some generations minimized the statement and called it idolatrous. Others revered it and called it normative. The question of the place of Mary in the history of salvation has ebbed and flowed throughout the centuries. But all of them have been formed by it in some way. It is, how-

ever, still a concept in process of development. And painfully so.

There is, as a result, another story, not apocryphal, not
humorous, that may illustrate the tension best, that highlights
just how unresolved the place of women can become when
the role of Mary is inadequately defined. The story reads:

> A former Milwaukee woman—wearing a white alb
> with a red cincture—briefly interrupted the ordina-
> tion of a Catholic priest to protest the Roman Catho-
> lic Church's refusal to ordain women into the priest-
> hood.
>
> A writer and playwright walked to the altar at
> the Cathedral of Christ the King when the male can-
> didate for the priesthood was called forward to be
> ordained. She told Bishop J. Kendrick Williams, who
> presided, "I am called by the Holy Spirit to present
> myself for ordination, too."
>
> Williams replied, "I understand your difficulty
> and that you are called. I feel your pain," he said,
> "and I pray to God for women like you."
>
> Later, during his homily, Williams spoke about the
> action. "Janice, of course, is going through her pain
> as many women are in the Church today," he said.
> Addressing the newly ordained he added, "I would
> be remiss if I did not point out to you that the divi-
> sion in the Church today will cause you pain also."[15]

Indeed there is pain aplenty. What does God really want
from women? What kind of a sign is Mary to us all? What,
if anything, do we see in her that has any meaning for women
today? I remember that as a young child, despite the efforts
of the nuns who taught me, the parish that formed me, and
the example of other girls my own age, I developed no devotion for the rosary. I found it very difficult, in fact, to say

one with any feeling at all. Mary simply did not appeal to me. She was, they taught me, docile and passive, submissive and unquestioning. She was not the strong, self-directing, thinking woman my mother was. What could I possibly find in Mary to respect, to imitate?

It took years but little by little the masks began to fall away and I saw for myself a Mary they never told me about but who, once I allowed myself to see for myself, was, yes, painfully apparent. I had to rethink everything to be able to see her. This was a woman who made up her mind outside the law, alone, independent of keepers or guides. This was a woman who risked everything to do what she knew her God required of her, whatever its cost socially, publicly, spiritually. This was a woman who acted alone, outside the permission of the systems and the tradition around her. This was a woman who inserted herself into a public situation and directed Jesus to do the same, despite the fact that he said he was not ready to do so. She had a strong will, a strong faith, a strong sense of self, and deep spiritual stamina. The contrast between what I was always told about Mary and what I found in the Mary I saw before me in the Scriptures has affected me deeply as a woman.

We say we respect Mary; but when it comes to dealing with other women in the Church, we make no association between the role of Mary in the plan of salvation and the role of women in general. We ask women to cook the church dinners, but we do not ask them to be diocesan consultants; we make women Sundy school teachers, but not church theologians. We buy statues of Mary and ignore the women at her feet. And, in the end, we deal with only one dimension of Mary's life as well. We concentrate instead on the virginity of Mary, ignoring the fact that even here there are issues to be resolved.

In the first place, the translation of the word "virgin" itself is in question. Saint Paul, for instance, who writes long before biographical details of Jesus' life begin to be inserted into the gospels for the sake of generations to come, explains to the Galatians simply that Jesus was "born of a woman" (Gal 4:4). The original Hebrew text of Isaiah—"a young woman will give birth to Immanuel"—as quoted in the Gospel of Matthew, does the same. Later translators, however, used the Greek word "parthenos" (virgin) for the Hebrew word "almah" (young woman) because in that culture at that time, a young married woman who had not yet borne a child, scholars now know, could still be called a virgin.

Even more confusing, if virginity itself was all so important to the claims of Christ—as the tradition came to assert—we have to ask ourselves why neither Mark nor John refer at all to either the birth of Jesus or the virginity of Mary in their own gospels. But we do. All the time. As if Jesus would not be Jesus otherwise. As if it matters to the nature and person of the Christ. We have, in fact, concentrated so much on the sexual dimension of the life of Mary and the birth of Jesus that we have all but completely ignored the implications of the Annunciation for women in general, and in particular for the place of women in the Church. We completely ignore, as a result, the need for the feminine dimension in life itself, not biologically but spiritually. We lose the gifts of half the human race. We forego the insights of half the human race. We miss the meaning of half the human race. And we blame it all on Mary, despite the fact that lurking under that excuse is a tradition of depth and challenge often overlooked, always minimized.

Mary's role in redemption is a revered tradition in the Church, officially articulated for the first time in the fourth century and confirmed in every century thereafter as the popular appreciation of Mary grew from "Mother of God" at the Council of Ephesus in 431[16] to "Queen of Heaven" by Pius XII in 1954.[17]

The truth is that our concentration on a "virgin birth" narrows our focus to a very small facet of Mary's life, of every woman's life. Mary was far more than a birthing mother. This may, as a result, diminish our perception as a people of the larger faith message being demonstrated here. We have instead, in our determination to make the virginity of Mary our focus, obsessed about sex, categorized people on the basis of their sexuality, and managed to divide even women themselves over the issue. We created a hierarchy of women. We distinguished between virgins and nonvirgins in ways that made one kind of woman better than the other, something we never did with men, for instance. We never—note: never—made male virginity the measure of a man's character and spiritual value as we did for women, though Joseph's virginity is part of the tradition, too.

This concentration on the virginity of Mary, rather than on the call of Mary to become a channel of divine presence, is dualism run amok. We have missed entirely, it seems, that the birth of Jesus "by a woman" may well be a metaphor for a legitimate, a necessary part, of the spiritual process for everyone everywhere, men as well as women. At all times. Even here. Even now. The place of Mary in the divine plan raises a question of major spiritual meaning for the Church: Can the fullness of the vision of God, the totality of the Jesus-message, possibly be achieved even today without the agency of women? How real is the birthing of the presence of God among us in the churches if women are not involved?

The questions challenge us to the very depth of our souls. Delimiting the role of Mary to a biological one alone completely ignores the other messages of her life and presence. It confines her meaning to one moment of her life and disdains the rest of it. We ignore the Mary who carried good news to Elizabeth and opened herself to the strong support, the wisdom, the guidance, the direction of another woman.

We ignore the Mary who did not take the message of the incarnation to the priests, to the rabbis, not even to Joseph, her spouse, for approval or for legitimation, but who received it herself and acted on it herself. We ignore the woman Mary who bore the burden of criticism, fear, and rejection but, full of the consciousness of God's call in her, never wavered in the faith that God was leading us to something new. We ignore our first model of strength, faith, conviction, and equality.

By concentrating solely on the Virgin birth, we run the risk of neglecting the implications for the development of the Church of the wedding feast at Cana. It is Mary who catapults Jesus into ministry there, and it is Mary who orchestrates the event. The woman who brought Jesus into a private world now launches him into the public one for which she bore him. And it is the woman who does it, not the apostles, not the rabbis there, despite the fact that we have denied women the right to direct the ministers of the Church ever since.

By fixing our attention solely on Mary's role as virgin and mother we reduce, if we even recall, the ramifications of her presence with the apostles at the descent of the Holy Spirit on them all. We forget, if we ever realized, that it is this moment that entrusts and strengthens them all to undertake the responsibility for the future of the Church through the guidance of the Spirit. We give women no responsibility at all for the sacramental, theological, or canonical development of the Church. What does that say about the spirit of Pentecost in us all?

Finally, we may be missing the most major Christian message of them all, even in our concentration on the virgin birth. We remember the Annunciation but we forget its central truth: Mary was not used. Mary was not made a pawn in the birth of Christ. Mary was asked a question to which she had the right to say no. Mary was made a participant in the initiatives of God. God did not impose on Mary. Mary was not treated by God, as women generations after her have been, as a means to someone else's ends. Mary did not have life forced upon her. She was made an equal partner in the process. God asked a woman a question, something that happened only rarely thereafter. Mary chose to say yes. To see Mary as some kind of passive instrument in the hands of God, for all its apparent piety, despite the facade of reverence it affects, simply makes Mary herself a sex object—a holy sex object, perhaps, but a sex object just the same. Given that limited point of view, Mary becomes a woman with no rights to her body, a serious departure from the Scripture scenario itself.

The fact is that the Scriptures give us a picture that is quite the opposite. Mary deliberates with the angel. Mary questions that angel. Mary, in a culture given to the total control of women, makes a personal decision and replies to the angel, takes the responsibility for the act, and bears the consequences. Mary is a strong woman who changes the course of human history, even reverses the nature of spirituality, as well as immerses herself in the Divine.

What's more, the titles "Mother of the Church" and "Queen of Heaven"[18] applied by the Church itself to Mary, imply just the opposite of the way the virgin birth has been traditionally interpreted. Here is a woman whose presence is essential on every level, who shares in the divine plan of salvation, does for the Church what the Church must do for the world: be the conduit of the Divine. In fact, without her it would not be. But that is not the model that has been presented for popular emulation. The Mary presented to women for imitation and to men as the ideal woman is passive, silent, and asexual. Mary, key figure in the Incarnation, the public life, the crucifixion, and the descent of the Holy Spirit is blurred into a single role, motherhood, and all women after her are viewed the same.

It is a sad affair for the history of the Church. It drains us of women in ministry. It denies us the voice of women in the interpretation of the voice of a God in Scripture that a woman bore for us. It robs us of the place of women in human history now.

Mary and the virgin birth are indeed the very proof we have that women are not simply sexual instruments in a sex-hungry world whose interests are more biological than spiritual. The Creed says that women do marvelous things, all of them far beyond the physical. The Creed makes the physical the way and not the end.

The Creed does not make sex contemptuous; it makes it natural. It puts sex in the service of the soul. It takes our mind off the sexuality of women, if we can only see it this way, and shows us woman in all her glory: woman rational, spiritual, strong, essential, decisive, and ordained to participate in the outpouring of divine life. It shows us woman—loving, giving, holy, in communion with God, and filled with the spirit of Jesus.

It is when we begin to see the virgin birth as separate entities—as virgin and as birth—that we lose sight of its greater meaning, its broader message. It does not say to me that "virgin" is better. It says that God does not see sex as what birth is all about and not what women are all about, either. It says that sex is not the way we should be defining women. "Birthing" is about bringing the Divine to life in us, however that needs to be done.

Until we can say "I believe that Jesus...was born of the Virgin Mary" and mean that a woman was spiritual partner to the greatest spiritual event of all time, then the devotion we have for her can only be partial and the pain that comes from that bent and biased preconception will strike at the root of the faith, make it lesser, and limit its growth.

SUFFERED...

When I was a young woman, I remember being very disturbed by the old Marian hymn that talked about "this vale of tears." What a thing to say about life, I thought, young and heady, full of possibility and impervious to reality. But as the years went by, and one disappointment, one loss, followed another, I began to realize that life was, indeed, "a vale of tears." In the end, there was no denying it. The record was clear enough: War had changed the world forever, on every level, in every category. An entire population of Jews had been exterminated in Europe. Millions died in Siberia. Whole peoples starved to death in Africa while the rest of the world watched on kitchen television sets. And from a personal standpoint, too, the struggle got clearer as the years went by: My own mother had been a twenty-one-year-old widow left with this three-year-old child in a period when there were no jobs for men, let alone for women. I myself had lain paralyzed and in an iron lung at the age of sixteen, one of the last victims of the last polio epidemic in the country. Work I wanted to do I did not get, and things I did not want to do I found myself fated to without consultation, without interest.

Those whom I thought were good friends either became distant or disappeared from my life entirely. People I loved dearly died before I really got to know them or lived in an Alzheimer world for twenty-eight years as my mother did.

Indeed, I have lived all my life surrounded by death, failure, disappointment, and struggle. This element of the Creed I understand. This element of the Creed I cling to for direction. And so, I believe, do all the rest of humankind whose lives are even more fraught and twice as enigmatic as any I myself have ever known. How do we understand it all? How do we reconcile the fact that this vale of tears is a terrible place and yet is not a terrible place at all?

One of the most fascinating dimensions of the Creed, I think, is the fact that the element of the Creed that is most clear of all is the element in the Creed that is most unclear in life. The Creed shows us suffering up close and real. Why?

The facet of the Gospel most historically sound, least metaphorically presented, is the passion of Jesus. There was, we know, from sources outside the Christian community as well as from within it, a man named Jesus who was crucified in Jerusalem under the Roman procurator, Pilate, in the reign of Tiberius Caesar. But that's as far as the evidence goes. Why he died, and with what meaning for us today, has been the subject of theological investigation, conciliar argument, and private speculation ever since. Every generation struggles to explain both the suffering of Jesus and suffering in general. The explanations often raise far more questions than they answer. But one thing is clear: Suffering is part of life, both for us and for Jesus, both for Jesus and for us.

Ironically, then, this may be the most important, the most acceptable segment of the entire Creed. Otherwise, how can we ask anyone to believe in a God who does not know the plight of being human? How can we be asked to bear what we have never seen borne well? How can we be asked to do what has no value whatsoever? The suffering of Jesus may be the one proof we have that Jesus was really human and that humanity, whatever its pain, can transcend the burden of it.

The ancient Church explained the suffering of Jesus as a kind of payment for sin. In the context of a feudal society

in which offenses against a Lord could only be really satisfied by a person of equal rank, if at all,[19] Anselm of Canter-
bury taught that humans had sinned against God. It would
take someone of the rank of God, then, to satisfy for such a
sin. Therefore, God sent Jesus to be sacrificed on the cross
for our sins, the new offering of the old Mosaic covenant
that had itself first been sealed in blood. The Son of God
would die to expiate for what humans themselves could not
possibly atone. But as acceptable, logical, necessary as that
model may have seemed for a society in which justice and
reconciliation was a matter of balancing equals off against
one another, this notion of what Jesus was about destroys
Jesus' notion of God. In this explanation, the God who demands the sacrifice of Jesus is not the God Jesus described.
The atonement model of God leaves us with a vengeful God,
an angry God, a manipulative God, a feudal God, or a mas-
ochistic God. Not the God of Sarah and Hagar, of Joseph and
Daniel. It leaves us bereft of the God who welcomes back prodi-
gal sons with fatted lambs and banquets, the God who counts
the hairs on our heads and feeds the sparrows in the sky. The
loving God who, when asked for bread does not give a stone,
is surely not the God who sends a son to be killed in some
kind of blood sacrifice designed to appease a divine ego.

No, I do not believe that God wanted Jesus crucified. I
believe that people wanted Jesus crucified, that what God
wanted was to provide a model of the God-life in our midst
which a world immersed in greed, competition, oppression,
and institutionalism would not accept. Jesus does not suffer
because God designed it that way. Jesus suffers because humans designed it that way.

The suffering of Jesus is a very human thing. The people
he came to love, the system he meant to stretch to its human limits, to its fullest potential, to its deepest vision of
God, turned against him. We have all known the situation,
the feeling, the pain. It is what people did to Jesus that killed

him. It is what the system did to him that destroyed him. It was a fearful system and apathetic people that brought the total sacrifice of Godhead to an ultimate end. It is what people did—or failed to do—for the One who had already sacrificed everything for our sakes, who "did not deign being equal to God a thing to be clung to but who became like us in everything," that led to his death. It is that outpouring of his blood, that sacrifice that the crucifixion crowns. This is the suffering that takes all the love a human being has. This is the kind of suffering that is divine mystery nobly, humanly, borne.

Jesus does not come to appease God. Jesus comes to teach us how to live a life that makes us worthy of the God who made us. Jesus comes to show us what we ourselves can be, must be. Jesus comes so that we can come to be everything we were created to be, whenever our lives, wherever our efforts, whatever our circumstances: shining glory or abject degradation.

The unfortunate tendency among us is to concentrate on the crucifixion alone when we talk about the passion of Jesus. But the Creed opens our eyes much wider than that. The Creed requires us to remember the suffering that preceded the death itself. It is the suffering of Christ that instructs, that gives us insight into our own lives, that lends us strength for our own journeys. Few of us will be crucified, of course, but all of us will, somehow, walk the way of Jesus before our own long days and lonely nights come to an end. The memory of Jesus gives us a choice: We can walk through the Golgothas of our own lives as he did, with the same understanding, the same steady faith, the same awareness of God's providence for us as we go, or we can stumble our way through, bitter and alienated from the very moments that, like his, can bring us to our glory.

To concentrate solely on the cross diminishes the Incarnation, reduces the sacrifice almost to ritual, and misses its larger meaning, its total context, the outpouring of divine self that came moment by mundane moment all the years before it. The cross simply cannot be understood separate from the life that preceded it. Jesus' death is not distinct from who he was, from what he was doing before the arrest, the mock trial, the rejection by the crowds. Jesus' crucifixion is not other than the Nativity. Jesus suffered far greater pains than death long before death was kind enough to take him. There was more to the purpose of his life than a Roman cross. It was the life he lived that led to the cross upon which he died.

The truth of the passion rings across time for each of us: The goal we each seek is the cross we each choose. The purpose of our lives determines the nature of our deaths. What we stood for in life determines who will be at our deathbeds, how we will be regarded by the "nice" people of the time, the degree of respect with which we will be held thereafter. Jesus lived the human cross with us, for us. We have a companion on the way.

Holy Week, that stretch of time between Christ's entry into Jerusalem for the feast of Passover to the laying in the tomb a week later, is a panoply of the sufferings and the heartaches that life brings to the process of the honing of souls. Christ suffers the disillusionment that comes with superficial success, a sense of failure, betrayal by people he trusted, misunderstanding by authority, fear, humiliation, abandonment, loneliness, despair, and death. And he shows all of us how to do the same. To say "I believe…Christ 'suffered'" is to say "I believe that suffering can be transcended." It is to throw in our lot with hope.

It is not simply the death of Jesus that is our redemption. It is every aspect of the life of Jesus that redeems us, that shows us the path of reconciliation, that becomes the Way beyond our small, bleak selves to the God who wants our Good, our immersion in Godness. The passion of Christ only unmasks the cost of it for one brief, tragic moment. The Creed does not glorify suffering; it simply records it so that we might never forget the glory of humanity taxed to the utmost for the sake of the reign of God. To say "I believe that Jesus suffered" is to say "I believe that suffering is not too high a price to pay for this God who is our Good." It is to give our hearts to commitment.

But hearts get broken along the way to God. There are simply too many possibilities for glittering delusion, for dismal defeat, not sometime to run headlong into the pain of the process. Christ has gone them all before us. Christ knew the applause of crowds fed for a day and mistook it for a change of heart. In front of the palace of Pilate these are the people who, paid a little money on the side, cajoled and coerced by the institutional types around them, called in the end for the release of Barabbas, the thug, rather than for Jesus the wonder-worker. They had no need for his wonders now. What they needed was approval from the government, security in the system. We learn from the suffering Jesus not to presume that anyone but God will be with us, either, at the end.

Christ suffered a sense of failure. "Hosanna!" they shouted on Sunday; "Crucify him!" they shouted on Friday. Scribes and Pharisees contested with him to the end. His own disciples were looking for posh positions in a kingdom he had no intention of creating. Who does not know the scene: We start out with such high ideals, all of us, and see them so often go to straw. The business does not thrive on fair prices and just labor practices; the ethical legislation we want, however hard we work, is defeated; our children run the streets and haunt the bars, drop out of school and leave our dreams behind, devote themselves to making money, and abandon their families, whatever effort we put into their upbringing, however closely we adhered to the perfect mother, perfect father patterns. Everywhere we look, nothing has bloomed as once we planned. We learn from the suffering Jesus that success is not what life is about. Life is about wholeness, not about effectiveness.

Christ suffered betrayal by the people he trusted most in life. His own family called him crazy, one hand-picked disciple defected when it counted most, collaborated with the other side, turned him over to his enemies when treason was more to his advantage than fidelity. We learn from the suffering Jesus that principles cost, that in the end it is, indeed, "everybody for himself" that is often stronger stuff than "I believe in you."

Jesus was misunderstood by almost everybody he met: his family, the apostles, the government, even the religious leaders of the time who should, it seems, have recognized him first and understood him best. Some wanted him to be a miracle man, others wanted him to be a military man, almost nobody wanted him to be himself. The crowds wanted cures that the synagogue did not want to have done on the Sabbath and that the rabbis associated with Beelzebub to begin with, since they weren't doing them themselves. The apostles wanted proof of who he was and a bit of prudence in his behaviors. "Don't go up to Jerusalem," Peter himself begged him. Don't go, in other words, where you'll draw official attention to yourself, Jesus, and get us all in trouble. Who doesn't know what it is like to be told not to talk about politics in front of the family or feminism in front of the bishop or abortion in the office or economic theory in the prayer group or peace rather than war at the party because those are all "private" matters. We learn from the suffering Jesus to risk the price of paying what the soul cannot ignore.

Jesus suffered emotional breakdown and physical exhaustion. He wept in the Garden, full of fear, depressed to the point of darkness and discouragement, awash in failure. It had all been for nothing. It had all been ignored. The

God who whispered in his heart all his life was silent now. There was nothing left. No confident gleam in the eye. No miracles for himself. No certainty of divine justification. Indeed, we understand the situation all too well. We know what it is like to lose everything, to have strength drain away and self-esteem die and in their place wash back only frustration and nothingness. From the suffering Jesus we learn that the end is never the end, that there is more to do, that we can get up and go on again.

Jesus knew fear and humiliation and abandonment and loneliness at the hardest moments of his life. The apostles slept in the Garden, Peter drew a knife, the Roman guards tore off his clothes, everybody—everybody—disappeared. No one spoke in his behalf. No one admitted that they even knew him. No one stood by while he died, except his mother, now a helpless widow, and the women—and maybe one of the Twelve, according to only one of the gospels. No lepers came, no cripples keened, no rich influential types pulled strings or bought a pardon, no protestors demanded his release. He died in disgrace, a criminal of the state. And he died without a curse on his lips. We learn from the suffering Jesus that life lived in concert with our God is, even at the moment of total destruction, the only strength we need to survive it, soul intact, heart unshriveled.

Jesus suffered. Those may be the two most human words in Scripture. They may also be the words which are, when life seems to have become a burden too great for each of us to bear, the two words that really save us all.

John Donne wrote, "Affliction is a treasure, and scarce any man hath enough of it."[20] Suffering erases our illusions. Then there is nothing between us and God. To say "I believe in Jesus Christ...who suffered" is to say that I believe that suffering is not destruction, and may, in fact, be the defining glory of our lives. I believe that the God who is absent is present to me.

15

UNDER
PONTIUS PILATE...

I was a young teacher in a newly built central high school. For almost a hundred years, a community of Benedictine Sisters had administered the parish school that had preceded this one. When the new school opened, the Sisters were simply transplanted to the new unit and a diocesan priest arrived as headmaster. I was junior home room advisor the year when the brightest, most socially active and most promising students in the class were inducted into the National Honor Society. As class moderator, I was responsible to see that it was done correctly.

The National Honor Society was the most prestigious organization secondary schools had to offer young women and men who were academically gifted. The value of the Society lay not only in its recognition of a youngster's present educational accomplishments but in its impact on their future options, as well. Students elected to the National Honor Society could almost assume they would get scholarships into colleges of their choice.

But in this place there was more than prestige at stake. The school was located in a rolling rural area in the foothills of Pennsylvania. It was a small town built almost entirely on what were now basically defunct oil fields. Some people were very poor. Few families were very rich. Every-

body in-between lived well enough, but they also lived carefully. They took good care of simple houses, they paid their
bills regularly, they drove new cars, but no one I knew took
anything for granted. To have a child inducted into the
National Honor Society took a great burden off the education budget in a town of what were usually large families.

Names of the nominees were kept completely secret until
the moment of the public announcement. Nevertheless, students were painfully conscious of the event and aware of the
stakes involved. To meet the social, public, and academic criteria required for consideration, they joined too many clubs,
stayed after school for too many activities, ran for class of-
fices and, tired as they were, kept assiduous account of their
grades. This year five places had been reserved for the school
by the national association that allotted the number of inductees on the basis of school size. The higher a student's place on
the list, the more likely was she or he to pass college entrance requirements or get financial aid. This year, there
were three girls and two boys who qualified for induction.

The day of the NHS induction ceremony, I went to school
early to make a final check of last-minute arrangements. The
headmaster had already put the names of the inductees in
faculty mailboxes, but the bell was ringing for first period
before I got around to scanning the faculty announcement
sheet. Suddenly, I stopped short. Then I read the paper again
and raced out of the faculty room. Somehow, a terrible mistake had been made. Instead of reading girl-girl-boy-girl-
boy, the list now read boy-girl-boy-girl-girl. Both boys' names
were now among the top three places on the list. I was beside myself. How could I possibly have made that mistake?
I found my grade book and went rushing in to the
headmaster's office to get the list corrected before the assembly began. "Father, there's been a terrible mistake. I don't
know how it happened, but the NHS announcement is
wrong." I opened the grade book to the page of cumulative

averages and pushed it across the desk to him. But he reached out his arm and propelled it back to me, gently but firmly. "No, no," he said, in a kind of avuncular way, clearly pleased with himself. "There's no mistake. I changed the order of induction." I gasped. "You changed it? How can you do that? Why?" He crossed his arms across his broad chest. "Because, you see," he said patiently, teaching me the way of the world, "girls don't need an education as much as boys do. And boys need role models to encourage them to study." "Oh," I said. "Oh." After all, it was his school. He was the headmaster. He could do whatever he wanted to do.

That afternoon, I sat in the back of the gym and watched my students inducted in the order he announced. Later that week, the mothers of the two high-ranking girls came to the school, grades and papers in hand. But the headmaster's order of induction stood, of course. And I watched it all and never said a word.

It took years for me to realize it, but Pontius Pilate and I became cohorts that afternoon. I began to see him through new eyes. Most of all, I never said the Creed quite the same again.

If there is an anomalous line in the Creed, "suffered under Pontius Pilate" is surely it. Out of nowhere, in the midst of a treatise on the depths of Christian existence comes a name. And a strange name, the wrong name, at that. The Creed does not list the names of the apostles, or the prophets, for instance. The Creed does not even name the gospel writers themselves on whose witness the Creed itself depends for authenticity. No, other than Mary, his mother, the Creed names only one person: the Roman procurator who ordered Jesus put to death. Why? To what spiritual purpose and daily use? In my own life, the answer lies layered in a cavern in my mind, silent and ashamed. On two levels.

The first reason for the blasphemy must, of course, be credibility. Pontius Pilate is the historical reality upon which the Creed relies for legitimization. Pilate provides the most obvious proof we have that the events surrounding the death of Jesus can be historically verified. They happened. They are not fiction. They are not fantasy. They are not the imaginings of religious fanatics. This is not a first-century rendition on a theme of kidnapping by aliens from outer space. Pilate did exist. He did order the death of Jesus of Nazareth. Documents attest to that. The death of Jesus lies ingloriously certified in the works of the Roman historian, Tacitus. The enemy acknowledges it, in other words, not only friends, not only those who might have wanted to use the death of a political martyr to rile up a politically frustrated people whose dignity lay in the ignominious dust of foreign domination. The death of Jesus is not simply the concoction of a small group of partisans who claim the death of an innocent man to unseat an unacceptable government. The man who ordered the killing admits it, as well. Interpret this death as you will, the Creed implies, but by all means, do not doubt it. Pontius Pilate ordered the itinerant preacher, the Nazarene, the wonder-worker, the "unique Son of God," the very one in whom he himself "found no cause" for execution, put to death. Why? And what does that imply for the rest of us?

Pilate himself must be reckoned with for several reasons. First, he was the Roman governor of the territory of Judea, an outpost, a crossroads of an empire that by this time stretched from the British Isles to Egypt, from Armenia to Morocco. No Roman governor was welcome here, but no Roman could be removed. The Jews were fodder in the face of Roman legions. Second, Pilate himself, last in a series of short-term Roman governors, all of them ineffective or despised, was at best suspect, even in Rome, where patronage had more to do with his appointment than merit or nobility. To the least politically adroit his moves had all the earmarks of political ineptitude. He had rung worship

images of the emperor throughout Jerusalem, of all possible postures the least likely to be acceptable to a culture
whose God was not even nameable, let alone perceptible.
He had coins minted that carried Roman religious symbols
in Jewish territory, a practice however common that was
nevertheless unacceptable to the Jews. His own reign, in
other words, stood mired in political quicksand and he was
desperate to hold on to it.

Later, the Jewish historian Josephus, who wrote under
the patronage of the Flavian emperors, would describe Pilate
as strong-willed, strict, and authoritarian, but politically
cunning. He had a history of going so far and no further.
He kept the Roman presence in the place established; he
collected the taxes and he damped the sporadic uprisings,
but he did not try to impose a Roman regime or the Roman
religion on the Jews. For that, the Jews had their own system. As matters would have it, however, this system was
weakening, too, in the face of this man whom some called
the "Messiah." Meaning a political warrior. Clearly, Pilate
and the Jews needed one another. Unholy truces may reek
more of self-serving than of either allegiance or beneficence,
but they work.

It fell on Pilate, then, to keep order in a place that had
been in foment, at the boiling stage, for years. He did it
with a heavy hand. He also did it according to the law. He
had here, in Jesus, they told him, someone whose influence
over the crowds threatened his own very tenuous position
and someone the members of the Sanhedrin would like to
see out of the way for the sake of their own political positions, as well. The marriage was an arranged one: The
Sanhedrin and Pilate brokered a very smooth political alli-
ance-of-opposites, a devil's agreement designed for the good
of both of them. The members of the Sanhedrin wanted to
maintain an orthodox community. Pilate was the governor
of a foreign territory who brooked no revolt, no warmon-

gering, no opposition parties. I have no doubt whatsoever
that the same kind of thing happened under American governors in occupied Japan after World War II. It happens
regularly on the death rows of each of the fifty states in the
union even now: Governors pass death sentences more for
political reasons than for moral ones.

Pilate was keeping Roman order in a foreign place. In
him all the weight of the empire came to bear on a simple
people fighting a guerrilla war of snide words and occa-
sional sabotage against the greatest power in the then-known
world. But before it was over, Pilate was a kind of victim,
too. Or if not a victim, surely a bellwether for the rest of us.
The story of Pontius Pilate is the human moment in the
Creed. It is our moment. It is the point at which we and our
lives come under the scrutiny of belief.

It is this second reason for the insertion of Pontius Pilate in
the center of the Creed that is, I think, far more profound than
the first reason—and far more disturbing. This one has nothing to do with history. This one has something to do with us.
Pilate inhabits the world around us at every turn and takes
each of back again and again to the throne of personal judgment. Pilate embodies all the base demands the world can make
on good people. Pilate makes us examine our own motives,
our own responses to everything, every day of our lives.

The story is an obvious one: Jesus of Nazareth comes
preaching a new kind of society, a new set of values, a new
model of authority to both the Temple and the Roman Tri-
bunal. The implications smacked of the unthinkable. The
challenge of change is hard enough for any system to contemplate. More ominous than the thought of simple organizational adjustment for Jewish leaders and an imperial
appointee, however, was the realization that the people who
walked the narrow streets of both the villages and the capital liked what they were hearing about this man, Jesus.
Galileans were following him in droves. City people were

watching him with great interest. Too much of this and the old systems would fall. In their hearts, both Pilate and the priests knew it was true. This man must be silenced, must be jailed, must be excommunicated, must be discredited at all costs. Must, if necessary, be done away with. "Better for one man to die..." the Sanhedrin had said, than for the whole system to fall because of him.

But how? Carefully, that's how. Pilate could not find anything in Jesus serious enough to condemn. Pilate's wife was so troubled by the image of the gentle Jesus that she dreamed about him and begged Pilate to avoid this case for his own good. The chief priests reminded him that Jesus threatened the security of the throne and might, in Rome, where things counted for Pilate, be considered treasonous. Worst of all, the crowds called for the release of Barabbas by executive clemency, rather than Jesus as he hoped they would. Pilate was in the middle—like we are so many times. Justice was on one side; expedience was on the other. System was on one side; righteousness was on the other. I remember it well: the struggle with "obedience," the deference to the system, the sacrifice of the innocent, the concern for approval. Most of all, I remember that I said nothing.

Pilate fascinates me. My fear is that I understand him. And worse, that he understands me, too. He's not a bad man. He's not even what we would call a weak man, if by that we mean a simpering one. On the contrary. Pilate does his work thoroughly and decisively. He is an agent of the state. He wants to be appreciated by the state. His future depends on it. He functions independently; he's not dishonest. But he steps very, very carefully. And always to his own advantage. When the chief priests provide the reason he's looking for—this man is treasonous—he chooses personal safety over personal integrity. This man may be innocent but the man threatens his own position; therefore, the man must go. We know the contest very well. Pilate lives in us, too, and refuses to sacrifice the self for the sake of the other.

Pilate is the part of my own heart that cannot make a decision, cannot stand against the crowds, cannot pursue truth above personal exigency. Pilate is the part of us that does not stand up for good, that fails to see human decency in the drifters, the condemned, the underside of our worlds. The Pilate in each of us puts to the test all the ideals we mouth everywhere else in the Creed. There is no doubt in my mind. For me, at least, Pilate stands in the Creed as stark proof that Jesus is not really safe with me. Not yet.

16

WAS CRUCIFIED...

I remember the cross that hung at the first landing of the monastery's chapel stairway only too well. It was far larger than life-size and it towered over us, heavy with a twisted, bleeding Christ. It filled the small space in a gruesome, uncomfortable way and made entrance into the bright chapel above it with its high stained-glass windows and gleaming altar a study in opposites. You could touch the contorted legs of the hanging Christ as you went by if you so chose, but I never saw anyone do it. This was a cross to avoid as far as possible. When I look back, I realize now that the history it conjured up was good, but the theology it implied was terrible.

The fact that crucifixion ranks as one of the worst ways a person can die stands on firm, sensible, psychological ground. The feeling that everything about that death was contrived by God for some sort of grim theological payback does not. Trying to get a balance between the two perspectives has been one of the most difficult spiritual struggles of my own life. Who beat this writhing, wrenching Jesus to a pulp and why? The God who loved him and claims to love me? Or someone else? And if someone else, what does that say about this cross, this life, and this God, as well?

Years later, when the community built a new monastery on a new spot, someone took that cross off the chapel wall and planted it outside in the center of the monastery prop-

erty. Whoever did it was either very smart or hardly smart
at all. The house-paint corpus, the untreated wood, decayed
quickly. First, the paint cracked and melted. Then, exposed
to one storm after another, one winter harder than the last,
the corpus sagged and broke.

The only thing left of the original crucifix in that garden to this day is a hunk of bare, black cross, ugly and
empty of a figure. As bad as that is at one level, perhaps, it's
not necessarily bad at all. The bare, empty cross teaches us
a great deal about the crucifixion, about ourselves and about
the God the Creed purports to profess. We so much prefer
to contemplate the spiritual life through candles and incense,
rather than through pain. But who has not hung contorted
on a cross? And who has not looked then at the cross of
Christ and been saved by it? And who has not as a result
been able to see beyond it to the day when, coming down
from the cross, it would be possible again for each of us to
rise to new life? And who of us has not found a cross worth
climbing and could still pretend to be fully alive? If there's
nothing worth dying for in our lives are we really living?

The problem comes when we get confused about how
Jesus got on that cross in the first place. The reason we
ascribe to the crucifixion can determine the rest of our own
lives. If we assume, as the Western world did, thanks to Anselm's
theory of Atonement, that the "sacrifice" of Jesus to appease
an angry and insulted God is the explanation for the crucifixion of Christ, then the spiritual life totters on the edge of becoming one long excursion into masochism. I had a professor
once who described that kind of negative spirituality as any
state of mind that assumes that "dancing is bad, drinking is
bad, hemorrhoids are good." It poisons life. It turns God
into a ghoulish keeper of human anthills, no better than the
tribal gods before us. I call the distinction one of the more
important lessons of my life. When I pull up anchor and
drift in the light of a sunset, when I eat pizza with friends,

when I listen to Tchaikovsky or contemplate Thomas Cole's *View from Mount Holyoke,* I say to myself, "No, this is not the God who put Jesus on the cross." Then what did?

My second-grade teacher frightened the life out of me with her explanation of the crucifixion, I admit. An implacable God required the death of Jesus, God's own son, because of my sins. I was undone by the thought of it. The Good Friday liturgy with its equally clear and completely uncompromising presentation left me cold for years. But the older I get, the more obvious those explanations become. What put Jesus on the cross? Sin did. The refusal of the human community to tolerate the reign of God here and now made the cross inevitable. The divine values that Jesus embodied, the cosmic vision for the world that Jesus proclaimed, the pinnacles of human development that Jesus made plain day after dusty day from the byways of Galilee to the top of the Mount of Beatitudes—love, mercy, peace, and justice—these are the principles that put Jesus on the cross. These cost. These accuse. These are the principles that keep Jesus pinioned there still, and made a laughingstock, or, worse, ceremoniously celebrated and ceremoniously ignored.

Love, mercy, peace, and justice—these are the apogee of human existence to which the Creed is calling us every time we pray, "I believe in Jesus...crucified." And they are no more acceptable now than then. Call for an end to military pulverization carried out in the name of foreign policy initiatives and see what people think of you. Call for life sentences for those on death row and see how people look at you. Call for demilitarization in the name of human services and see how fast you're accused of being unpatriotic. Call for public day-care centers, wage equity, standardized promotion policies, and universal health insurance instead of abortion and see what happens then to the proclaimed concern for women's rights. Call for a distribution of wealth in a world where profit, power, and personal freedom are the gods of the day and see how quickly you lose your place at the tables of the rich and the powerful. Call the Church to discuss the question of women's ordination and see how long you are considered pious. Or, more to the point: Cure lepers on the Sabbath, forgive adultery, refuse to bear a sword, contest systemic evil in both church and state, cure a woman with a hemorrhage of blood and see how long you last in society. These are the things that put people on crosses. These are the things the cross is all about. The Pharisees did not want Jesus breaking the Sabbath. The elders did not want men punished for adultery as women were. The apostles did not want to surrender to the Roman soldiers without a fight. The crowds did not approve of the bleeding woman who broke ritualistic taboos and touched the hem of Jesus' cloak. Neither the priests nor Pilate wanted to risk a social revolution in behalf of the poor and dispossessed. The cross, in other words, was the inevitable end—for Jesus and for anyone else who does the same in the face of an intransigent system.

The Creed tells us that in Jesus the reign of God became present, became apparent—and, all the while claiming to be saved, the human community refused it. But that is not the only tragedy of the crucifixion. We pray regularly, "I believe in Jesus—crucified" and then refuse to take up the same cross ourselves. More than that, we go on refusing it daily—in the name of God—as if we can just settle down now and, immersed in private pietism, take as our basic spiritual goal to get through life with as little trouble as possible so that we're not caught short on Judgment Day. It is a totally self-serving kind of religion. That approach does not follow the crucified Christ. It simply reduces religion to a series of symbolic gestures designed to make me feel good, righteous, and, above all, safe. That kind of thinking makes for us a god who sits and waits for us to make a mistake. It's the adoration of a god named "Gotcha." It's a pagan god. That kind of thinking enables me to ignore my place in the universe, my role in co-creation, my purpose in life, my very relationship to the God who created me. The cross of Christ is the call to our hearts that reminds us that nothing ushers in the dawn of God except living it. But it's not that easy. A commitment untested is no commitment at all. But who wants the promise of the cross? Who wants the rejection? Who wants the foolishness? Who wants the risk? Not I. And yet without it, the Creed goes flat.

Holiness, the crucifixion shows us, is not so much a matter of not doing evil as it is a matter of doing good. Salvation is a gift, but it is not a gift without substance, without challenge, without personal responsibility. No matter how much we liturgize, how much we pray, how much we cry, "Lord, Lord," the rest of salvation depends on us. Salvation demands that, like Jesus, we do our part to bring the reign of God now. The lepers are waiting for us now to cure them. The blind are looking to us now to give them sight. The Pharisees are questioning us now for answers to the question, "Is this the One who is to come or shall we look for another?"

The cross reminds us daily that God did God's part: Jesus came and, in him, God showed us the Way. We have, then, all been saved. We have been saved from our delusions about what is really important in this world. We have been saved from our fear of risking disapproval here. We have been saved from our sense of nothingness in the face of God because God walks the way we all must walk. We have been saved from the right to claim darkness of soul and uncertainty of vision. The fact is that we know very well what we are expected to do because we have already seen Jesus do it. All that is needed is that we become publicly what we purport to be privately and that we become privately what we purport to be publicly. Private piety is not enough. It is at best only half the journey to Jesus. In fact, private piety is what we so often seek in order to justify our lack of raw, clear Christian commitment, the kind of commitment that puts a person on a cross. When Jesus said, "Follow me," Jesus was really saying that salvation is incomplete until it lives in us. The truth is that people put Jesus on the cross, God did not.

The problem, of course, lies in having to go on trying to bring the reign of God when the reign of God does not come, whatever our efforts. We work on behalf of the poor, and every year there are more hungry children. We struggle for justice in the working place, and more and more companies every year institute part-time work schedules to avoid paying the social or medical benefits required for full-time employees. We send money to peace groups, and the country goes to war regardless. We beg musicians and liturgists and parish priests to use universal language, and they laugh at us and do nothing. Isn't it time, I ask myself, to give up, to admit that none of these things is ever going to happen, to realize the fruitless and foolish and silly idealism of them? Isn't it time to listen to music or read a book or spend a week in the woods communing with God and nature? Maybe. But not forever. Not for always. Because the minute I do, they get up in church and say the Creed. "I believe in Jesus…crucified." Then, I remember the crucifix at the top of the chapel stairs and the blackened cross in the monastery garden, and I know that one demands the other. To stop the bleeding in the world around me, I will have to take one more person down from the cross. It's then that I wish I had had the courage to touch that corpus as I went by. Maybe I would be more ready, as a result, to touch it where I see it around me now. Maybe then salvation would be real for both of us—me and the person out there now who is waiting, waiting, waiting for someone to take them down from the cross on which they hang hoping for salvation. Theirs and mine.

DIED, WAS BURIED
AND DESCENDED
TO THE DEAD...

There is nothing in the world like the closing of a grave. I remember the whole process so well. It was early in the evening of Christmas Day. The rest of the world was ending the celebration, but we had not even had Christmas dinner yet. My father had gone across town to visit his brother until I could get through all the scheduled events of the day: the liturgy, a community punch bowl, Christmas dinner for a widower and his five small children. Then, when it was all over, at the end of the afternoon, we would finally sit down together for our own family moments. I could smell the stuffed chicken all through the house as the hours went by. It was 9:00 p.m. before I heard my mother in the kitchen turning off the oven. My father was now three hours late for Christmas dinner. In fact, he never got there at all. To this day, I can still hear my mother's scream.

After hours of working on him, the hospital finally called to inform us of the accident. He hung on for awhile, of course, but little by little the last grey ghost of life ebbed out of him, against all exertion of the human will, despite all the tricks of modern medicine, in the face of all the technology and machines and shots and surgeries and lab tests the

world had to offer. It was a desolate time: my father in a
coma; my mother alone, probably, I knew, for the rest of
her life. The night he died, I walked out of the hospital lobby
stunned and angry, my mother on my arm and not the glim-
mer of a notion about what to do next. The street teemed
with moving, swaying crowds. Why were all those people
still talking? Who were those young men across the street
who dared to laugh? When would those cars stop and let
the world take its moment of silence? As it should. As it
must. But no one stopped at all. The world simply went on.
This great death, I discovered, was not on the world's agenda
at all. It was in my own heart alone, bare and raw. No one
else even noticed. It is those moments, I realized in the course
of his funeral mass, in which we cling to "died, was buried
and descended into death." At those moments, the Creed
becomes more a lifeline than a litmus test of belief or a liturgical nicety.

Jesus was born, yes. That we take for granted. But "Jesus
died"? And "was buried"? And "descended into death"?
Now that is something to contemplate. Theologians have
debated for years the possible meanings of both renderings
of the phrase: Did Jesus descend to "hell," into Sheol—the
realm of the dead—or, in the words of medieval theologians
centuries later, did Jesus descend into "hell," into Gehenna,
the place of the damned? No one knows for sure, they are
honest enough to admit. Both traditions, in fact, have long
histories in the Church. Eastern theologians interpreted the
phrase one way, Western theologians another. Eastern theologians, always more mystically inclined, tended to think of
it as a moment of cosmic proclamation of God's justification of humanity in the person of Jesus, the Christ. Western
theologians—Cyril of Jerusalem, Augustine, Thomas
Aquinas—on the other hand, more rule-bound and legalistic by nature, thought of it as the release of the dead from
sin.[21] But, frankly, as theologically interesting and intricate

as the ideas might be, when it comes to the meaning of life—when it comes to funerals of the people we love—who really cares? The point is that Jesus died and was buried and went among the dead, died the way we do—and that makes all the difference. If Jesus died, after all, who are we to escape it? And if Jesus did not escape it, what need have we to fear it?

The best proof that the interpretation of how and where Jesus went after death is at best peripheral to the human condition may lie in the very fact that the phrase "descended into hell" began to appear in the Creed relatively late. During the Arian controversy—those debates in the Church that centered around the nature of Jesus, divine or human—various local churches took a stand for the humanity of Christ by stressing in the Creed the fact of his death, meaning the hallmark of life. The phrase appeared first in fourth-century Syria, then in some Spanish creeds in the sixth century, then in the Gallican liturgy in the seventh and eighth centuries, and finally into the Creed of the universal Church in the Middle Ages.[22] The point became clearer and clearer, more and more a matter for recognition in the daily life, in the spiritual repertoire of a soul in search: The death of Jesus had been authentic. Real. Human. Terrible. And its corollary the same: None of us escapes death. None of us.

But why not? Why death? Why not simply a series of assumptions: yours, mine, everybody's? Creation could certainly have been fashioned as easily that way as this way. Why not just leave this world pulverized into glory right in the face of the ones we love? Why the loss of life, rather than its clear and quick transformation? No answer is sure, of course. Faith is still faith—belief beyond reason—if for no other purpose than that there is a great deal that begs to be understood and nothing better to believe about it. Faith, after all, is what makes sense of what we don't know and can't comprehend and need to discover. From the perspective of faith, then, death has a very spiritual purpose. We go through the end of life to life, I am convinced, for the same reason that Jesus himself went through death: so that those who stay behind, impaled by the starkness of an end time, have no choice but to stop and take stock. We go through death so that life can become new over and over again, so that over and over again, we can see the lives of those around us with new eyes. We struggle with the consciousness of mortality, perhaps, so that we are forced to drop off the clouds of our thunderous ambitions and implacable egos once in a while and examine our own life from the perspective of its dissolution. We interrupt the liveliness of life to deal with the deadliness of death so that whether we choose to or not, we come face to face again with the presence of the God in whose womb we live and breathe and have our being. Thanks to death, we survive the disease of creeping invincibility and open ourselves to learn something about life as we go along. Death gives life to life. At each death that means something to us, we grope our way back to the meaning of life — and change our own.

Death affords the counterpoint, the descant to life. Death teaches us that all things end, that many things fail, that God's time is not our time.

The finality of death rises as stumbling block to many. But it is difficult as life goes on not to see it as grace gone wild. If nothing ever ended, nothing new could ever begin. The losses that we thought would surely kill us are the losses that reorient our lives. When we lose something that has consumed us, we discover aspects of life we long ago ceased to realize we even had. "I'll never marry again," the woman said to me. "The marriage I had was wonderful, but now I have other things I want to do in life."

Death is an exercise in "enough is enough." Death points to newness of life, for those who stay behind as well as for those who go. What death ends, in other words, it also begins. Painfully, perhaps. Fearfully, often. But never without new challenge, new gift, new opportunity. It's when we shutter up the windows of our souls and hide behind yesterday that tomorrow never comes, no matter how long we live.

The death of Jesus left a fledgling faith community bereft until they themselves rose out of his grave to begin life over again, wiser now for what they knew, stronger now for what he was, determined now to finish what had already been begun. All things end so that something else can begin.

But the death of Jesus signals more than the end of mortal life. It guarantees as well the human capacity to survive failure. The death of Jesus makes failure real, makes failure bearable, makes failure holy. Jesus hangs on a cross to remind us that he failed—in both the synagogue and the state. Jesus did not succeed—at least not the way it seemed that he would. And neither will we. Ask anyone who has lived long enough, given themselves to something deeply enough, worked at something hard enough, depended on something totally enough, and the pattern is plain. Failure is part of the process of succeeding in the ways that count most.

Jesus failed with the people; they deserted him. Jesus failed with the synagogue; it rejected him. Jesus failed with the apostles; they slept through the rising tide of betrayal; they ran away under pressure when he needed them most; they let him die alone, undefended and unthanked; they lived in fear when it was courage that was needed. We know the feelings. Children abandon their homes as much as parents abandon their children. A life's work crumbles under the attack of success as well as the despair of inadequacy or the shock of accident or the miscalculation that comes with misadventure. What worked is destroyed by factors over which we have no control. Jealousy erodes the good. Resources run out before the project ends. Energy runs out just as the attempt poises to succeed. Indeed, there are a thousand ways to fail. Someone else comes along and gets the credit. Someone else comes along and changes course. Someone else comes along and erases the footsteps in the sand. Whatever way it happens, the moment of realization that the great enterprise of our lives is over grinds a sense of purpose out of life. We lie on the empty field of life, alone and ignored after years of support, and wonder what, if anything, it has all been about. Only one hope remains: that the Jesus whose grave was found empty, will also empty ours.

Jesus, the Great Failure, breathes life into every broken moment. And takes the fear away. And dampens the anger. And smiles. Time to begin again. Time to watch the waves roll in late, but strong and just from whence no one expected the backwash to come. The function of failure as Jesus shows us so clearly is to prove to us that, really, in the end, nothing fails at all. The only thing that can fail is our ability to believe that nothing in life is wasted, that it will all come to some good end, sooner or later, with us or without us, whether we can see it or not. To say, "I believe in Jesus Christ...who died, was buried and descended into death" is to say, "I believe in God's own time."

The Scriptures are very clear about the birth of Christ. "When all things were in the fullness of time," Paul teaches us, "the messiah came" (Gal 4:4). The only thing wrong with that insight is that we forget it too soon and contemplate it too little. We forget that it has as much to do with failure as it has to do with success. Time goes by and nothing seems to happen. Until the fullness of time. Until all things are ready. All we can do is to contribute to readiness. And wait for it. In God's good time the drop of water that goes into the stream today will reach the ocean. In God's good time, the work we start in life will come to full—no matter who interrupts it on the way. In God's good time, the tomb will empty.

The "fullness" of time is the moment at which all things are in place to enable something to happen. Leonardo da Vinci imagined the airplane centuries before engines existed to power them. Louis-Sebastien Lenormand fashioned the first parachute centuries before there were airplanes. Dorothy Day went to jail time after time to bring the attention of the Church to the barbarity of war. It was decades and several wars later before the United States bishops wrote a peace pastoral. None of them saw what they spent their lives to achieve. Did they fail or did they succeed? It all depends on how you view the tomb of Christ. Sometimes it is only failure that shows us what success could really look like.

"How many snowflakes does it take to break a branch," the White Dove asked the Snowcloud. "578, 972," the Snowcloud answered. "Ah," said the White Dove, "What if we only needed one more voice to speak before peace could come." Success is not a matter of doing something perfectly. It is a matter of doing it until the time comes for it to happen, until God's time is fulfilled. In the meantime, what is necessary is simply to leave the tombs of our lives and go on waiting.

ON THE THIRD DAY, HE ROSE AGAIN FROM THE DEAD...

I watched it happen. She'd been the attentive young bride, the perfect mother, the professional wife. She'd done her internship but gave that up to follow the man to another country, to work in a variety store to pay bills while he finished school, eventually to have the first child, and finally to settle down, a stranger in a strange place. It was a life of playgrounds and dinner parties, of ironing in front of TV sets while he lectured, and of planting the garden or driving the children while he took his trips, did his research, wrote his books.

Then, one day, she changed the pattern. She went back to school, too, started a business of her own, began to give a few lectures herself. She was no longer home to cook big meals anymore. She went away on weekend trips, developed a circle of friends, embarked on her own projects. For a while, he was stunned, lost, hurt, and angry. He'd been the perfect husband and it wasn't enough for her, he said. She was hurt. She was also confident—and determined. She'd been the perfect invisible wife, she said, and he couldn't understand that she wanted also to be a person.

It was a very private revolution. No one heard a sound. It happened in silence, in secret even. But it was cataclysmic. Little by little, of course, life took on a new shape for both of them. Things stabilized—eventually. They each forgot as time went by who they once had been, either alone or together. And yet, nothing was ever quite the same again. She was transformed and it changed him, too. She rose from one life to another and it made demands on him, too. She was not a new person, she said, just the one she'd been all along. She didn't really "change." She just became in full what she'd always known herself to be, and he had finally begun to realize it. It was a rocky time for both of them, but an exciting time as well. They each became new people again. I watched the transformation between the two and came to understand the Creed a little better. Actually, what I really came to understand better was the process of transformation. And, I am convinced, if you have never experienced transformation, you can never really begin to understand resurrection either.

For most of my young life, the image of Jesus rising from the tomb was just that: Jesus died and came to life again, I thought. And no one disabused me of the concept. But it troubled me, I must admit, even as a small child. I plagued religion teachers with questions: Where was that body now, I wanted to know. I spent hours looking up into the sky, thinking that if I looked long enough, someday I'd surely see it. But if it was someplace up in the sky, why didn't it fall down? And if God was pure "spirit," how could Jesus be body? In fact, why was Jesus body at all? I didn't learn much about Jesus in the process, but I did learn not to ask those kinds of questions. I learned to recite the catechism and keep the problems to myself. I learned that the silencing of thought was far too often what adults called "faith." And I learned years later that it is just such "faith" which, in the end, stands to stamp out faith completely.

Actually, the facts were far more sensible than the explanations: The early Christian community, at first stunned
by the loss of Jesus and paralyzed by fear, suddenly experienced the cataclysmic, too. All of their normal expectations
had been shattered: The burial was not normal. Few of the
crucified were buried at all, historians tell us. The entomb-
ment was not normal. The itinerant preacher Jesus was, if
he was entombed at all, put in a rich man's grave. And now,
their own experiences were not normal, either. They had
seen him again. They found themselves more deeply immersed in Jesus than ever before.

"The tomb was empty," the Scriptures said later, metaphorically perhaps but pointedly, nevertheless. People had
known his presence again, not the same as before the crucifixion, true, but real, nevertheless. Transformed. Somehow
or other Jesus had defeated death, had snatched new life
from its cavernous throat. The implications were overwhelming. Death, even once transcended, could never be perma-
nent again. In fact, life itself could never be the same again.
Jesus risen from the dead made life the stuff of eternity. Jesus
transformed leads us to look beyond the obvious, to allow
for the presence of God in alien places in unanticipated ways.
Resurrection begs the scrutiny of the obvious, the celebration of the sacrament of transformation.

The question is, of course, what really happened there?
And what does it have to do with us? The answer is simple.
Transformation happened. What had always been became
more of what it was. And because of that, life changed everywhere. The transformation was on both sides: Jesus
waxed to new fullness, yes, but so did the people around
him. New life burgeoned everywhere.

Where once they had known Jesus, in retrospect people
now saw the Christ, the anointed one of God for whom
they waited, as well. There were witnesses. Women first,
then the disciples, then people on the road. But, most inter-

esting of all, they each saw him differently now: Mary Magdalene did not recognize him in the Garden. The disciples on the road to Emmaus never realized who he was until it was almost too late and then, more by what he did than what he looked like. Thomas identified only the wounds. The presence of Jesus had somehow or other been transformed among them. Things were clearly real, but things were just as surely changed.

He did not live with them now: he simply "came" to them. He did not do the things he did before. He showed a new semblance of himself—or if not really new, at least largely unnoticed before this time. This radiant Jesus had always been there, had even been glimpsed from time to time, perhaps, but had never before this been fully luminous, completely effulgent, totally aglow, entirely apparent to the people around him. That we understand. We know that growth and change are not death. Clearly, Jesus had not left them. Jesus had become what Jesus was meant to be. And that we understand as we grow, as well. Jesus gladdened, graced, and recharged the world around them as always. But differently.

One thing for sure: The Resurrection of Jesus is not about "resuscitation." A corpse does not come to life here and wait again to die. A body does not rise to bleed again. After the crucifixion, Jesus "appeared" in places, the Scripture tells us. He did not walk through doorways. He did not travel to them as he did from Galilee to Jerusalem. He did not sail to them as he did to Capernaum. He did not ride there by borrowed colt as he did on the way to the Temple. He simply "appeared" in the midst of their lives, while they were doing mundane things, without warning but vividly, the same but different. No, the Resurrection of Jesus is not about revivification of an old life, it is about experiencing a new kind of life entirely.[23] And no one knows how it happened; we only know that it happened. They "saw" him and "heard" him and "walked" with him and felt his presence in their lives. What else is there to know in a world where the wondrous has become commonplace? We "see" people and "hear" people and "experience" people long gone or far away and do it routinely and take it all for granted. Here, too, an entire community began to experience Jesus differently.

Resurrection testifies to the metamorphosis of the Jesus of history to the Christ of faith. It is about the shift in people's perception of the Jesus of first-century Nazareth to the Christ who galvanizes all time. It is about the Incarnation of the Jesus born in Bethlehem to the Jesus born in us. It designates the transformation of the Jesus who rises from the dead in Jerusalem to the Jesus who rises, if we allow it, in us. The Resurrection of Jesus is about coming to grips with the transformed and transforming presence of Christ then, now, and always. Once that happens, life is never again the same. Life begins anew.

To say, "I believe in Jesus Christ…who rose from the dead," then, is to say I believe that the Resurrection goes on and on and on forever. Every time Jesus rises in our own hearts in new ways, the Resurrection happens again. Every time we see Jesus where we did not recognize him before—in the faces of the poor, in the love of the unloved, in the revelatory moments of life, Jesus rises anew. But that is not all. The real proof of the Resurrection lies not in the transformation of Jesus alone but in the transformation awaiting us who accept it.

To say, "I believe in Jesus Christ…who rose from the dead" is to say something about myself at the same time. It says that I myself am ready to be transformed. Once the Christ-life rises in me, I rise to new life as well. "Christ is risen; we are risen," we sing at Easter. But it has a great deal more to do with life than with death. If I know that Jesus has been transformed, then I am transformed myself and,

as a result, everything around me. Transformation is never
a private affair. But it is always a decisive one.

The Scripture is quite clear: It was "on the third day"
that the Resurrection happened. To the Jewish mind it was,
in other words, a time of great cataclysmic evolution. Our
culture calls such moments "Rubicon" events, times of decision, moments of momentous change. Jewish culture in-
dicated them by dating them "the third day." Scripture, in
fact, identifies thirty defining events—occurrences the result of which the Jewish community, Jewish history, or Jewish understanding of the ways of God on earth were never
the same again—as having occurred on "the third day." On
"the third day," for instance, God seals the covenant with
Moses. On "the third day" Esther goes to the King to beg
for the safety of the Jews. On "the third day" Abraham
prepares to sacrifice Isaac.[24]

To speak of something as having happened on "the third
day," then, signals a crossover moment in time, a point
at which everything before and everything after is seen in
new light. The Resurrection happens, Scripture says, "on
the third day." The message is clear: No one and nothing is
the same after the Resurrection happens. Jesus may have
changed after the crucifixion, but the Resurrection changed
the rest of the Christian community, as well. Transformation is like that. When one person changes so must everyone else around them. Resurrection changes us as much as
it changes Jesus.

Until we find ourselves with new hearts, more penetrating insights, fewer compulsions, less need for the transient,
greater awareness of the spiritual pulse of life, resurrection
has not really happened for us. Jesus has risen but we have
not. Resurrection is about transfiguration. Life as we once
knew it, defined it, shaped it—if we really believe in the
Risen Christ—rises redefined. Transformation in any of us
calls the rest of us to transformation. Change changes eve-

rybody. Relationships shift. Expectations alter. Insight deepens. We begin to see as we have never seen before.

Resurrection is change at the root of the soul. It marks a whole new way of being in life. But there is another dimension to resurrection, too, that pierces dailiness to the heart and makes of the Creed a mantra to possibility. "On the third day, Jesus rose again," we pray. "Jesus rose again," and so must we.

The real lesson of resurrection may be its strangest, strongest one. When Jesus died, hope died. The apostles grieved the death of Jesus. The public was scandalized. The synagogue said good riddance to a troublemaker. The entire enterprise collapsed. But in the end, out of apparent failure, came new life stronger than it had ever been before. And so, too, for us. When one phase of life ends, a new one arises, if we do not spend too much time grieving the one before it, if we allow new grace to flow through us, if we accept the fact that "the third day"—the moment of ultimate incidents—is an ordinary moment of time turned Christic, turned salvific, turned new. Resurrection strikes failure to the core.

HE ASCENDED INTO HEAVEN AND IS SEATED AT THE RIGHT HAND...

By popular social standards, she was a pretty pathetic figure. I never knew the young Sister Hildegund. I remember only the old Sister Hildegund, a deaf, bent-over, crone-like figure, an old German nun out of an old German mold. She raced through the halls far faster than her years allowed, busy from morning to night, talking to herself as she went, in a monastery where people walked on tiptoe and where silence hung over the long narrow halls and high-ceilinged rooms twenty-two hours a day. She never whispered, she only talked, and when she did try to comply to some prioress' admonition, people heard the hiss of it rooms away. Tell her something and she never heard a thing, but leave her with the cat in the basement and she never missed its cry for milk.

I worked with Sister Hildegund in her coif room, a corner section of her bare bedroom where she pleated and bricked and stacked the head linens she made weekly for a community of almost a hundred women. No one envied me the position.

She may have been a sweeping figure in her day but not when I knew her. I knew only the Sister Hildegund who sat bent over at her coif machine, chin sunk against her chest, her big knuckled, bony hands in constant motion. Every hour she took a brief recess, reached for her large-print Bible on the stand by her coif machine, traced her fingers along the lines, squinted through her thickset glasses, and read one passage over and over again till, it seemed, she was satisfied that she had swallowed it. I watched the process out of the side of my eyes, listening to her with great amusement.

The communication between us was a strange one. She muttered to herself all day long, shook me by the elbow when she didn't like the looks of the coifs I'd made, and taught me the process of medieval coif making by simply repleating a good number of them herself, saying with disgust over and over again as she redid them, "Jack rabbit. You jack rabbit,"—which, I soon discovered, was the lowest thing she could call a person. Very seldom did she bother to look at me directly. Sometimes I wondered if she even knew which novice it was who sat at the second machine with her every Saturday. But as the months went by, I began to understand her constant murmurings the way a person gets to understand a foreign language.

One day I realized that she was not talking to herself. She was talking to me, constantly, a veritable stream of instruction about religious life and prayer that ended always with the sound of a question mark. I learned to nod and grunt back. She never stopped to hear an answer. This was not a conversation. It was wisdom talking. And what she always talked about, I came to realize years later, was the God within who lifted us up above ourselves and stretched our vision beyond now to everywhere, to time eternal, to total justice and complete care. I know now as I look back on those scenes that she had learned this line of the Creed very well and used it to feed her deaf life to such a degree that she never deafened her soul. Sister Hildegund had a rich interior life, centered on the Jesus whose Ascension into heaven took all of us with him, beyond the limits of one kind of life to the limitless dimensions of another. Sister Hildegund saw that there was more to life than life. She contemplated it, she raised this one always to a level higher than it claimed. She lived above and beyond the narrow limits of her limited life. She may, in fact, have been more in touch with the rest of life than anyone else in the community.

The rest of us were totally centered and consumed by the substance of the present. Hildegund lived far beyond it. From her I learned the freedom that comes with ascending to a plane of life beyond an implacable present. From her I learned that to say, "I believe in Jesus Christ...who ascended into heaven" is to say "I believe in the mystical dimension of life...."

Only one evangelist, Luke, talks about the Ascension as a separate dimension of the life of Christ. Only Luke, in Acts, dates it "on the fortieth day." That the Resurrection proved Jesus' identity with God the other evangelists took for granted. They link the Ascension to Easter itself. But Luke has another lesson in mind. Jewish students studied with a rabbi "forty days," a symbolic number meaning the amount of time it took them to learn the master's teachings well enough to be able to repeat them.[25] To Luke, then, the time after we experience the Resurrection may have less to do with Jesus than it does with us, with the centering of our minds and hearts on the world and the work at hand. To acknowledge the Resurrection, to be raised to a new understanding of Jesus ourselves, in other words, requires the fashioning of a life of contemplative awareness.

The last line of Luke's Gospel reads "They returned to Jerusalem (after he 'was taken up to heaven') with great joy and they were continually in the temple praising God." Jesus is gone but not gone. Jesus has left them but not left them at all. They remember the Jesus of history, yes, but they live now immersed in the Christ of faith. Their minds and souls are raised to new awareness, to new insight, to new consciousness of the power of God among them. They have learned the teachings and are about to live them out themselves. They become contemplatives, those who plunge themselves into the quest for the mind of God, those who seek to see the world as God sees the world, those who see more to the world than simply the world.

The contemplative life, the mystical moment, lies shrouded under centuries of confusion, misunderstanding, misnomers, and inventions. A world in the grips of the newly defined eighteenth-century mechanistic model of the universe saw everything in terms of cause and effect, mover and moved, parts and systems. Education was broken down into the smallest parts and components. Science became a mad search for the atomic particle that contained the first and final, ultimate and singular secret to the composition of life. Even the spiritual life was defined in steps ranging from the purgative—the withdrawal from the material accoutrements of life in favor of more spiritual existence, to the unitive—that point of spiritual development where there existed perfect union with God. The process was charted. The spiritual life was a ladder to be scaled one stage at a time, from purging asceticisms to perfect union with God. As a result, the spiritual life became the domain of professionals who retired to cloisters where, the thinking was, only God could gain entrance. There, completely centered on the "spiritual" life as opposed to "the life of the world," a person became "contemplative." No other way.

There is a serious problem with that spirituality. It counts most of the world out, in the first place, and, in the second place, it completely discounts Jesus himself. The truth is that the Jesus who himself raised our hearts and minds to heaven, who told us that He himself was the Way, who said, "Those who see me see the Father," lived a life totally involved in the world around him, totally attuned to the heart of God, completely consumed by the Will of God for the world. That Jesus, the contemplative Jesus whose hidden life led him back and forth down the dirty, people-ridden roads of Galilee, raises the hearts of the disciples to heaven, true. But then, in Luke, while they stand fixed and in awe of the sight of Jesus-with-them, Jesus-gone, the angel asks these heaven-struck apostles, "What are you doing looking up to heaven?" Then, the voice of the angel within them sends them back to Jerusalem, a link between the two inseparable dimensions of life—the physical and the spiritual—full of the power of what they had seen eyes up to heaven and heads full of the teachings of Jesus, enough to fill a lifetime. Anybody's lifetime.

The point is that contemplatives are not fakirs, gurus, or professional religious types. "Contemplative" and "cloister" are not synonyms. Cloister is at best only one of many vehicles to contemplation, needed by some, irrelevant to others who see the face of another Jesus in the poor, the rejected, the starving, the beaten, and love it dearly. To call only one of these "the contemplative life" is to overlook entirely the contemplative dimension of all life—the life of the mother who feels the presence of God while bathing her baby; the life of the man who feels God's breaking heart in his own when he sees young soldiers walk by, the lives of old people who have spent all their lives doing good so that the reign of God could finally come, the lives of young people who offer themselves up for the love of another on altars of their own.

Contemplation has to do with seeing life as it is, not

with escaping one to find another. Contemplatives are ordinary people who are extraordinarily conscious of the impelling life of God both within them and around them. They live under the impulse of the God who made them and listen to the small, deep voice within that guides them from the crucifix of Christ to concern for the vastness of a creation not made for them alone. The contemplative sees the meaning of eternity in every moment in time.

The contemplative life is a life of awareness, sacramentalism, and divinization of the daily. The Jesus raised up on the cross is the Jesus also raised to realms of glory and the fullness of God. The contemplative knows as a result that there is no place where God is not because the contemplative has learned to see God everywhere. God is in suffering, and God is in glory. God is in the cosmic, and God is in the crucifixions of daily life. To the contemplative, the mundane is the stuff of immortality. The daily is the residence of the Divine.

Awareness, the first mark of the contemplative, brings us face to face with the holiness of life. Dualism with all its separation of spirit and matter, heaven and earth, reason and feeling, light and dark lies to us about the nature of creation. Life is not two substances—one spirit, one matter; one good, one evil—joined together on the tether of a fragile human breath. Life, the Creed teaches us in the Jesus who lived, died, and was experienced again, is two dimensions of one creation, integrated and brimming with the Divine in one another. "See these hands, look at these feet, touch these wounds," the Risen Christ says and yet manifests all of them now in a new dimension, the magnitude of which "eye hath not seen nor ear heard." And yet some have.

To the contemplative the entire world is sacramental. Everything speaks of God. Everything unveils God to us. The true contemplative is a naturalist, a lover of life, a respecter of persons, a diviner of the tangible who sees behind the masks of creation to the Creator.

Dailiness is the stuff of contemplation. The contemplative does not go looking for stardust in which to discover God. The contemplative sees God in the clay of the day. Here in the struggles of marriage and unemployment, of dissension and jealousies, of rejection and the broken shards of trust, the contemplative sees the Jesus who showed the way beyond the crucifixion to the Ascension, beyond suffering to the glory of wholeness.

Jesus came to be among us, the Creed sings. Jesus walked the earth and blessed it. Jesus lived the life of the living and grew in "wisdom, age, and grace" here. But Jesus raised our eyes above and beyond the narrow limits of our paltry little lives, showed us other horizons, gives us a world beyond ourselves. In the end, out of the dregs of the worst the world has to offer, the Creed lifts our eyes and our souls to the vision that transcends the pedestrian. The Creed brings us face to face with the mystical and reminds us to abide there all the while we walk the streets of the world.

Sister Hildegund bridged those two realms so well we hardly understood her at all. She didn't need to hear the rest of us to be happy, and in her deafness she was crying out to me to listen to the same, to see the same, to pursue the same as she did. The lesson came late but the lesson came, eventually, loud and clear. The Creed was right, she proved to me. "Jesus ascended into heaven and sits at the right hand of God" and I can, if I look hard enough at everything in front of me, find him there.

HE SHALL
COME AGAIN...

L ike everyone else, I suppose, I've prayed this line of the Creed into the ground. It trips so swiftly off the tongue, passing and gone before we can even realize the implications of the line. Too lightly, perhaps, to command the consideration it deserves. But I have discovered, from time to time, that of all the phrases of the Creed this one may be the showstopper of contemporary life. I have seen its underlying elements in operation over and over again. The first time I became conscious of the concepts that undergirded such a facile announcement of the Second Coming of Christ, I was taught by a child. The second time, a few days ago, I found myself struggling again with a memory that plagues my sense of self and simply will not let go of my psyche. Each incident left a new layer of meaning where once only words had been.

The first event was, to all intents and purposes, a very simple one. When I was a young sister in the community, the practice was for each of us to take an inventory of possessions at the beginning of every Lent. The prioress reviewed every "Lenten List" herself and annotated them, as well: "No one needs eight coifs," she would write in the margin, or "Sister, please take all personal books to the library as soon as you have finished reading them." The practice fell

into disuse as time passed, the remnant of an era long over-
due to disappear, for obvious reasons: Clothing wasn't uni-
form anymore, needs were a matter of personal circumstances,
books were particular to people and ministry, "things" were
no longer seen as the incontrovertible enemy of community
life. The exercise was well intentioned but without substance.
Worse, it was a waste of time. But Lent was not. The notion
of "enoughness" was not. The idea of personal control was
not. So, to give Lent a new kind of meaning, we instituted
the notion of a "Community Giveaway."

The "Giveaway" called the community to two kinds of
personal asceticism: the control of excess and its counterpart, the temptation to niggardliness. Some of us had too
much; some of us couldn't bear to throw anything away.
The answer, it seemed, lay in finding a way and a time when
we could give to people who needed things more than we
did. The process was a simple one: Packing boxes were put
at the top of each residence hall on Ash Wednesday. During
Lent, sisters went through trunks, cupboards, desk draw-
ers, and closets to identify items they no longer used or
wanted or felt they should have and deposited them, one by
one, in the boxes in the hall. Then, on some bright summer
day when the weather could be trusted and crowds could
gather, we held a prayer service about poverty and freedom
and trucked the boxes to the parking lot adjacent to our
inner-city soup kitchen.

On this particular day, the parking lot overflowed with
boxes and people. We had set up long tables to sort and
group and display the things. Inside the soup kitchen books
of six "shopping coupons" were passed out with each bag
of food distributed at the food pantry that day. Then the
culling started. Framed pictures went first, then music, then
shoes. I watched it all through eyes squinting against the
sun, squinting against a few warm tears, as well. Old men
rummaged around in the stacks of clothing for jackets and

shirts. Old women took scarves and bedclothes. Young mothers took housewares. Children took stuffed animals and tiny trinkets. We stood behind the tables to help with packaging and to take the tickets designed to assure that everyone got an even share.

Suddenly, a small boy appeared in front of my table. A little man, I should say. The children of the poor, children who have parented their parents, raised their younger brothers and sisters, been moved from one place to another so often, eaten so little, become adults so quickly. His arms were full. He had three blouses, one large-framed picture of woods in wintertime, a pair of boots, and a small plastic camera. "Sister," he said, "where do I get an extra ticket? I need to get something else." I counted the items. "Sorry, fella," I said. "Everybody gets to have six things only. You'll have to put one of your pieces back." Fair is fair, after all. "But I can't," he said. "I need them all." I got a little firmer. "Well, love, so does everybody else," I said to teach him one of the great lessons of life. "So we can't do that. You'll have to make a choice." "But it's my mother's birthday," he insisted, pointing to a ring case in his hand, one of those "faux diamond" gimmicks that attract the unwary and naive. What some nun was doing with it I did not know and could not guess. "I want this for a present for my mother," he insisted. His young eyes found mine and fixed there. "She's never been married and she needs a ring!" I looked cautiously around the parking lot, looked from one small clutch of people to another, all of whom needed more than we had to give them. Then, I dropped the ring case into the bag with the other six items. He never flinched, never begged, never doubted. He knew he needed it. He knew I could give it to him. He knew that if this place was what it purported to be, he'd get it. The child taught me the kind of hope the Creed had been trying to teach me for years.

But there is more to the phrase "He will come again"

than hope. There is a streak of frightening reality in it as wide as the heart is faithless. I have learned that one the hard way, too, in things both great and small. It embarrasses me yet to remember it. As a young teacher I slapped a child who, by the time I got done insisting that she concentrate, was far too nervous to complete the problem she did not understand. I have never been able to forget her face, to undo her fear, or to completely repent my violation of her person. Over the years, she has taught me a great deal more than I taught her. The memory never goes away.

Strangely enough, I know every time we recite the Creed that the two incidents years apart—the arithmetic lesson and the ring, guilt and hope—are of a piece and that the Creed has an answer to both of them.

To say "I believe in...Jesus Christ who will come again" is to wrestle with hope and come to terms with guilt. Neither term of the equation is necessarily easy. But, ironically enough, one feeds the other. And has, apparently, for centuries.

The Book of Daniel in the Hebrew Testament makes a symbolic statement about the relationship of Israel to its enemies and the downfall of its foreign oppressors. "A Son of Man" will come, the book proclaims, who will save Israel from the beasts that pursue it. The incident that prompted the book, scholars tell us, is very likely historical. Soon, however, it began to be applied to the world at large. In the End Time, Israel knew, Yahweh would send a savior to establish, finally, a kingdom of justice and peace. Those who had been faithful would be saved. In this scenario, oppressors are punished and good triumphs over evil. The righteous are rewarded, order is restored, Israel rises triumphant. To a people vulnerable on every side, soon could not be soon enough.

To the band of disciples schooled in messianic literature and left waiting in Jerusalem after crucifixion, the time was

now. Jesus would fulfill his promises and complete the time
of waiting. The early Church assumed a purposeful but brief
preparation time before the quick return of Christ.

But things soured. Christ did not return. Some clung
desperately to the idea that the waiting time would be short,
that this world stood doomed to be short-lived, that judgment was impending and fearsome. A few would be saved.
Many would fall. Armageddon, the great battle between
good and evil, loomed in the not too distant future, and
those not purified, not ready, would be forever lost. It was a
hoary picture, full of fire and damnation, that raised its head
with every disaster century after century to come. For many
thinkers, theologians, and pietists thereafter, plagues, wars,
and natural tragedies all signaled imminent judgment, all
called for rigorous asceticism and incessant penance. To this
mentality, God the Judge waited with watchful eye, damnation at the ready, for every straying heart, for every feeble
soul. So much for the Christ who cured the lame in a society that called sickness God's punishment for sin.

Concentration on the threat of judgment has marked
every century since, either more or less. Montanists in the
late second century called Christians to withdraw completely
from an evil and polluting world to prepare for the impending Second Coming of Christ. A few denominations to this
day make the Second Coming of Christ the focus of their
religious concern, some almost to the point of obsession.
Millennialists posit the end of the world at the end of every
century. In each case, linked to the prediction of the Second
Coming, are predictions of harsh and unrelenting Final Judgment. The picture is dour.

Of all the segments of the Creed this one has inspired
the most passion, the most fantasy, the most bile. In the
question of the Second Coming of Christ, the hopes and
guilt of all humankind come to a furious boil. Which Christ
will come: the avenging Christ—the theologically con-

structed Jesus whose perfection demands perfection—or the Christ of adulterous women and possessed men, of hemorrhaging outcasts and traitorous apostles—the historically authentic Jesus who went from one end of Israel to the other, forgiving, and forgiving, and forgiving.

The explanations shift and change, rise and fall from century to century, depending on the social situation, decided by the theological climate of the time. So what is left for the person who believes in God a loving Creator and the Jesus who casts out demons on a Sabbath? The answer is deceptively simple and unbearably obvious: The answer is hope. Only hope. Holy hope.

Faith we understand. Faith is adherence to what we believe must necessarily flow from the goodness of God but do not understand. Love is response to goodness. Love we grow into a little at a time as the goodness of life becomes more and more apparent. Love, we learn if we live long enough, hovers in the hollows of life, looking everywhere for the One who is everything. Faith is a perpetual journey to more. Love is a colloquy with the love I feel but cannot see. But hope stands rooted in the certainties of a future hinted at by the past but yet unaccomplished. Hope whispers within us like a soft, steady draft of daylight that what we believe in we shall attain. Hope leads us around dark corners looking for the grace of the moment, confident that God's will for us is good. Hope is a child with seven presents and six tickets waiting for redemption.

To say "I believe...that Jesus will come again in glory" is to say that hope is alive and well and feeding on faith in God's presence and love for God's life in the world. We nourish hope on memory: Knowing that we have always had in the past whatever it was that we needed in order to survive, to endure, to see, to be more than we ever thought we could become, we claim the right to expect it in the future. We see the judge, but we do not fear the judgment. We expect the judgment, but we trust the Judge who knows the clay in the center of our souls.

The Christ in whom we hope we have known among us. The God in whom we trust has the heart of the Jesus who forgave sinners who sinned repeatedly, who fed the hungry until they were full, who touched sinners and embraced enemies and listened to women. This is a God who sees the heart and knows its directions.

Hope and faith are inextricably linked: If I believe in God the Creator, then I must hope in this God's commitment to the eternally ongoing process of Creation. I am not born finished. I do not live whole. I do not die complete. There must be more. How? Who knows. When? Who cares? All we know is that we do not know the end of the black vastness in which we swirl, and that alone gives us hope.

Hope is not escape to a domain of fairy tales and myths designed to save me from an admission of my insignificance. I do not despair in my smallness. On the contrary, I bet my very life on human smallness. My puniness is not the best thing the universe has to offer. I place my trust on the fact that, indeed, everything is bigger than I am, that there is so much more to know, that I am living in a world which only thirty years ago was science fiction and today is fact. What is there about God that I cannot safely believe and confidently take hope in when only recently I didn't even know that quarks existed, or that talking from one side of the world to the other would someday be commonplace. Anything is possible; and Jesus, as far as I am concerned, is the best possibility of them all.

We are, of course, only punctuation marks in time. We are atoms in a universe of giants. But we are, at the same time, full of a life that refuses to die, endures though pathetically weak, and manages to find the human condition infinitely funny. The conclusion is piercingly clear for all the fuzziness of the data: We who are worth being born must be worth being brought to fullness. Somehow. Somewhere. Someday. Or Jesus was all for nothing. And creation is all for nothing. And we are all for nothing. But there is no one on earth who really believes that creation has no purpose. Why? Because everything that they themselves do in their infinitesimally minor moments of life is full of direction, reeks with intent, pulses with eternal meaning. How can we possibly assume less of God?

This is the segment of the Creed that lifts our hearts above the paltriness of the things the world teaches us to put our hopes in—riches, power, people, and even religious practices designed to save us without our having to do anything ourselves—to the one hope that does not die. We hope not to dissolve into nothingness because God is everything. We hope not to be disappointed in life because we know that life is more than what we see. We hope not to despair in the face of decay because body and spirit are one. To those who argue that flesh is evil, the Creed says "I believe that Jesus who dissolved into God...will come again in glory" to celebrate our own dissolution as well. Human hope rises in the face of defeat and says "God is, therefore so am I."

No doubt about it: We live in a giveaway world, laden down with gifts we did not expect and cannot buy—each of us, like the child, wanting more, for all sorts of good reasons. Most of all, we know, in the crevice between our minds that accuse us and our hearts that beat in hope, that the God who gave us our beginnings and the Jesus who lived through our yesterday will surely, surely give us a new kind of tomorrow as well.

21

TO JUDGE
THE LIVING
AND THE DEAD.

Every Friday night before Compline the community gathered for the Chapter of Faults, an ancient monastic practice known in Latin as "the scrutinium," the canvassing of the human soul to scour it from human sin for the sake of human growth. Older members of the community sat through the thing impassively deaf to what had been years of the same, most of them with an open book in hand unaware and uninterested in what was going on around them. Younger people sat stiff and rigid, hands under scapulars, eyes riveted to the floor, nervous and tense. I listened to every word of every person.

It was a highly ritualized event. We "spoke fault" for spilling water, for wasting pins and paper, for getting spots on our clothes, for making mistakes at prayer, for walking heavily in the halls. And then, with a nod at authenticity, for "faults" peculiar to ourselves—for breaking a dish in the kitchen, for scorching napkins in the laundry that week, for talking after night silence. When it was all over, the prioress pronounced the penance. I was there the night one of the novices in my novitiate ended the list by speaking fault "for standing on one leg." How else? I thought to myself.

What else would a person stand on if not a leg? Then I felt the laugh begin at the bottom of my stomach. My chair shook under the rattle of it. I heard people shifting in their seats to find the sound. Under the strain of trying to keep control, the pressure in me built, exploded, and pierced the heavy silence, a booming sound in a hollow place. I covered it with a hacking cough in the middle of summertime but knew that I had just heard one of the silliest—and most enlightening things—I'd ever encountered.

The whole affair had been a lesson in judgment, the worth of which served me in good stead for years. Some things are simply not worthy of human moralizing. To reduce religion to trivia demeans the God we say we seek. What's more, it shrivels the human soul to the consistency of tinfoil. It explains how people can go to church every Sunday, be proud of their participation in parish life, and think nothing whatsoever of calling the indiscriminate extinction of civilians by modern military might "collateral" damage. I knew as years went by that it was one thing to confess slapping a child; it was another to regret "standing on one leg." We had so confused the moral, immoral, and the amoral by that kind of introverted narcissism that our souls had lost tune with the greatness of God. "Thank God our time is now," Christopher Frye wrote, "when wrong comes up to face us everywhere…(and) Affairs are now soul size."[26] Frye was surely right. There are some things too paltry to be part of human soulfulness.

Religious communities long ago stopped such practices, long ago saw the superficiality of them, long ago grew up morally, spiritually, and psychologically; but the memory is not useless. Few of us ritualize spiritual childishness now, but all of us are subject to infantile notions of sin, judgment, accountability, and morality. I did not laugh in that scrutinium years ago because sin is not serious. I simply had the unconscious sense to laugh because sin is so serious that we ought not to confuse it with things that are laughable. We must learn to take nothing seriously but sin when we are talking about sin. We cannot fear the Last Judgment for "standing on one leg." Sin is far too important for that. The question is, what is it?

Most interesting of all the interpretations of the Creed, but almost lost to history now in the wake of the historical development of private confession, the rise of individualism, and the notion of particular judgment at the time of death, is the Jewish notion that the judgment of God would be on the nation, or on humanity as a whole, not on individuals. It was the Jewish nation as a whole, the Jewish people in general, who, according to the biblical tradition, were responsible for witnessing to Yahweh rather than to pagan gods and who would as a people, therefore, be held accountable for that life trust.

When the prophets spoke, they spoke to an entire people gone awry—not to individuals. They indicted the entire nation for taking on ways of godlessness and failing to remember the covenant, not simply individuals in the throes of internal struggle. To the Jewish mind, the private sins of particular individuals were real, but part of the process of living and growing. To this day, the Jewish confession of sin at Yom Kippur is a community recitation of individual failings of which we are all capable, not a private accusation of isolated personal sins. To a Jew, we are all sinners but the law of the community guides us to our best selves. "Blessed are you, Lord God of Israel, for giving us the Law," the Jew prays, because the law saves us from ourselves, guides us where we would not have the vision to go, brings us to become the best that we can be. To the Jewish mind, the Law is a blessing.

The segment of the Creed that calls us to remember judgment, then, is not a call to fear, it is a call to growth, to right-mindedness, to fidelity of direction. It is a call to the human community and a reminder to the individual. We are reminded by the thought of judgment that we must make hope real. We have not been created only to come to glory but to bring with us to Judgment Day our own portion of the reign of God. We are expected, the Creed implies, to prove our accountability, both personal and communal, to God's hopes for humankind.

To hope for the reign of God—for the justice and peace that mark the will of God for the world—is to pledge ourselves to do everything we can to bring it where we are. Now. Here. To hope for the reign of God is to put ourselves under its judgment, to make it the criteria for our own merit, to give ourselves to its getting. Judgment is the side of hope that demands participation in the bringing of God's will for the world. God does not save us unless we save ourselves.

The judgment of humanity, of the individual human soul, has something to do with having left creation better than when we first received it. God waits for us to finish God's work. Those already living in the reign of God create the reign of God around themselves, those devoted to fullness of life, achieve fullness of life. Those who have abandoned a commitment to the reign of God to live out a hope based on human gods—on wealth and power, on religious practices and social prestige—lose it. Surely the return of Jesus will be marked by one question: Were you for me or against me? Were you with me or not?

The implications of hope are major. What was really important in a communal society was that the community itself never forget its obligations to God. What we as a society, we as church, hold as values determines the canons that shape and drive the individuals within us. The nation that lowers its standards of justice and mercy, integrity and human dignity, is far more guilty than the individual who is lost in the swamp of them, alone and unguided. A church that fails to be the Jesus it preaches and the God it proclaims is corrupt at the core without doubt. Nevertheless, in the face of the cry for social responsibility, the individual stands in the dock as well. Each of us goes into the presence of God alone, armed only with the things we hoped for and what we did to bring them to our own times.

Hope, therefore, is not the whole story of what it means to wait again for Jesus. Hope in a world that has the capacity to destroy itself is an egg on the edge of a cliff. Someone, everyone, is responsible, together and alone, for hope's surety. Each of us bears the burden of its future. In a nation forever poised on the brink of military force, the humanity quotient of the world rests on the shoulders of those who distance themselves from responsibility for the action or applaud its merciless use. I've wondered repeatedly what Americans mean when they say they will support bombing raids on other countries only if we "intend to finish the job." Which means what? Will we call ourselves Christians, say we wait in "hope" for the coming of the reign of God and the return of Jesus, and agree to use military force only on the condition that we pulverize a nation, level its cities, liberate its women and children who are already at the mercy of one force by scorching them to charcoal by another. And all for the sake of winning a showdown between politicians? When does the liberator become the oppressor? At what point of anguish do we say enough? And for how much of the decision are we each responsible as we wait in "hope"?

The fact is that all of us live with the images before our eyes of those we've hurt, each of us tastes the guilt of our curdled little private wars in the back of our throats. Each of us has cooperated with violence, ignored evil, temporized with the gods of this world, and prayed the Creed at the same time. In the light of the pain we have ourselves inflicted, what right do we have to hope for good for ourselves?

Ironically enough, perfectionism is surely not the answer. But guilt may be. Perfectionism assumes a point beyond which there is nothing else to learn in life, nothing else to do to gain the reign of God. But guilt creeps into the core of the heart, recurring again and again, reminding us again and again that we were meant to be about better things. Until finally we relent and grow. The Creed invites us to consider our guilt and call it grace.

The nice thing about guilt is that it proves that we are still alive. If we can still feel moral angst, we can feel everything else in life, too. The first sign of healthy guilt is that we never feel guilty for the wrong things. Guilt always has something to do with failing to recognize my creaturehood or hurting someone else. Of the Ten Commandments, the first three have to do with recognizing that God is God and not making ourselves the center of the universe; the next seven have to do with doing harm to others. Nothing else counts. Not really. The question that measures guilt is always, *who was harmed?*

The second sign of healthy guilt is that it is not exaggerated. Spiritual vision is the ability to see things as they are. Some of our struggles are serious; some of them are not. Some of our moral arm-wrestling matches of life are longstanding and need to be uprooted; some of them are only momentary breakdowns in an otherwise well-ordered soul.

The third sign of healthy guilt is that we do something about it and put the situation behind us. The purpose of guilt always is simply to enable us to recognize where we are failing the coming of the reign of God so that we can do better the next time. Its purpose is not to leave us wallowing in the past. Never to feel guilty for anything I've done is to be a spiritual child. Always to feel guilty for things without substance is to be a spiritual invalid. When we follow the life of the Jesus who is the ultimate judge of life, when we examine closely the laws he broke and why, we begin to see what is really important. Then we become concerned about the really big things in life: the outcasts of society, the poor, the children, the handicapped, the women, the foreigners, the helpless, our own dearth of spiritual development, our own reckless indulgences, the lack of self-respect that leads me to devalue others. If we ever developed a sense of guilt about these things, we would have a completely different world.

Guilt, of course, can be a very distorted concept. When we spoke fault for "standing on one leg," people were marching in the streets outside the monastery for Civil Rights and desegregation. We did not, as a community, walk with them because, we were told, "good" sisters did not go out of their monasteries and convents. Why? For the sake of spirituality, of course. For the sake of contemplation. For the sake of going to the Last Judgment perfectly ready—perfectly distant, perfectly disinterested, perfectly removed from the human condition. It was a system that, full of good will but ignorant of the demands of hope, completely distorted what the coming of Jesus, both the first and the second time, was all about. And all of us do it still. We refuse to respond in the face of injustice, in the building of the kingdom, because we say it is better not to upset people, not to cause "division," not to challenge the system, not to mix religion and politics. But to say we believe in the coming of Christ to judge the living and the dead and to base that judgment more on private piety than on public commitment to the upbuilding of the beatitudes—the measuring stick of the One who will judge us—rejects the reign of God and reduces all of life to one gross and shallow mime of the Chapter of Faults.

Perfectionism depends on human standards of ritual and response. Judgment depends on a new attitude of soul, of putting on the mind of Christ—mercy and peace, justice and humility—of becoming what we hope for. Then, the judgment of which the Creed speaks gains cosmic importance, becomes soul-stretching, is worthy of a life.

I BELIEVE IN
THE HOLY SPIRIT...

We were sitting in a bare and hollow conference room in Cuernavaca. On one side of the table sat a bishop whom Rome was trying to pressure into resigning because of his work against the government in behalf of the poor. I couldn't help but note the irony of the situation: After all, when the pope opposed communism in Poland, they called it Christianity and him a great leader. When bishops opposed poverty in South America, they called it communism and an improper intermingling of church and state. This bishop showed no signs of the wear. He was a strong and imposing figure.

On the other side of the table sat a catechist, a political refugee from El Salvador, a woman in flight, running for her life because she had carried Scripture from village to village, teaching peasants to read the gospels as calls to liberation. She was a slight little woman, quiet and perhaps traumatized, I thought, but very, very determined.

We, on the other hand, were gringos, do-gooders down from the North who cared about the poor but did not live with them, and loved the Church but had never challenged its commitment to be as just as it purported to call others to be. What was the resolution to these opposites: "We must take hope. We must live in the Spirit," the bishop said. "God created us, Jesus leads us, and the Spirit will show us the Way." Maybe, I thought. But not necessarily. I couldn't help but remember the last religion class I'd been in before my confirmation, long past but not forgotten.

The parish priest had come to the class to make one final examination of the candidates, to make sure that some poor dumb kid didn't say the wrong thing in front of the bishop and, I know now, bring into question the orthodoxy of the parish, and maybe even of the parish priest himself. We sat on bleachers along the basketball court, a bunch of kids squirming our way through puberty, while he fired questions at us. Things were going very well until he asked the tricky one: "Why are you a Catholic?" he said. That one was not in the book. The class of choleric, shifting, pre-teens got very quiet. Finally, a tall boy shouted from the last row, "Because I believe in Christ." The priest raised his eyebrows and smiled a little, amusement around the edges of his eyes. "No," he said, looking across the seats for someone to give a better answer than that. "In order to get to heaven?" a bright but timid little girl beside me said. "No, no." the priest said. A terrific admission, I thought to myself, since another answer in the list of required items in the confirmation exercise said quite clearly that this was "the only true church," the implications of which were pretty clear to anybody who could read. If you wanted to go to heaven, you bloody well better be a Catholic.

"Come on. Somebody," the priest prodded again. "Because I know that this is the one true church," another boy said with great confidence. "No, no, no," the priest said, true to his earlier position. "Why are you Catholics? Think!" he said—more firmly this time, weighing his words and pushing, I was sure, for an answer that was not in the book. "Because I was born Catholic," I said boldly. "Right!" he boomed. "Right." You could feel the shock such a simple truth made on young people more geared to answers than to the implications of them. "You are Catholic because you were born Catholic. And now you will receive confirmation, and the Holy Spirit will be in you, showing you what that means for the rest of your life."

I've never been able to forget that moment. "Being Catholic" was something I would have to learn as I went along; and something inside of me, Holy Spirit, would tell me what it was meant to be. Years later, I came to understand that the priest was right. Being Christian is not a catechism exercise; it is a learning process, a testing of the circumstances outside ourselves against the spirit that is inside ourselves. But it is, I have discovered, a very dubious gift when the answers outside and questions inside are in conflict. Indeed, "God creates us, Jesus leads us" and the Spirit shows us ways that are not always in the book.

Confirmation, the sacrament of the Holy Spirit, thunders the arrival of courage and the recognition of gifts given to each of us, the apostle Paul says, for the good of the whole Church. Confirmation, it seems, is a kind of ordination of the laity. A rite of passage to full membership, full adulthood, full responsibility in the Church that despite the theology of it—I have learned over time as the priest predicted—never comes for women and only sometimes comes for men.

I remember it well, the church decked in red, the local bishop arriving in pomp and glory, the sponsors coming to swear that their young candidate for the sacrament was steeped in the faith and ready to fight to the death for it, the organ swelling, the conferral of a new name to mark this newly enspirited life, and finally the bishop's light tap across the candidate's cheek to remind us of the cost of living out the promptings of the Spirit within. And there it was: grace to defend the faith. I began, as I got older, to realize how difficult this thing was going to be.

Did the grace conferred and the gifts given equip us,

require us, to defend the faith even from the Church itself
as we went about now, the Holy Spirit and we, learning
what it really meant to be a Catholic? What was meant to
prevail if and when full membership and full spiritual adulthood and full responsibility ever came in conflict? What
exactly is required of the individual in situations when the
voice within is clear but the world around us is not yet ready
to hear it? Or worse, when the Church itself is not ready to
hear.

The Holy Spirit, God's energizing presence among us,
the life force that drives us beyond ourselves, that whispers
us into the great quest within, that makes life alive with a
purpose not seen but deeply, consciously, stubbornly felt
even in the midst of chaos, even at the edge of despair, sounds
the truth in us that we are more than we seem to be. Life
does not begin and end with us. There is more than we know,
there is an electric charge animating the world at every level
and, most of all, within. Holy Spirit suffuses all of life, calls
us into the mystery that is God, reminds us of the model
that is Jesus, brings us to the fullness of ourselves. Holy
Spirit is the great anti-gravitational force that calls us out of
somewhere into everywhere, that keeps us moving toward,
through, the black holes of life, certain that on the other
side of them is light, waiting and wishing us on.

Do I believe in the Holy Spirit? You bet I do. Nothing
else makes sense. Either the Spirit of God who created us is
with us still, either the presence of Christ who is the Way
abides in us in spirit, or the God of Creation and the Redeemer
of souls have never been with us at all. God's spirit does not
abandon us, cannot abandon us, if God is really God.

It is not difficult to believe that "holy spirit"—Scripture's
less specific, less personal term for this divine energy that is
more life force than ghostly presence—stirs the waters
around us yet, just as it hovered over the waters in the act
of Creation. At the same time, it is sometimes difficult to

believe that "holy spirit" is believed at all. What I really believe is that the Holy Spirit is the most active, least honored presence of God in the Church.

The Holy Spirit merits a lot of talk—but very little real respect. The theology of the Holy Spirit is relatively straightforward for a concept that is logical but not scientifically verifiable: The Spirit of God permeates the world and lives in each of us as an ongoing call to the Christing of the universe. We are each gifted, we are taught, in behalf of the ongoing creation of the world. What is hard to believe, therefore, is not that God permeates the universe with a presence that empowers all of us, but that the Church itself really believes that the Spirit of God truly infuses, really gifts, is really enfleshed in the human heart, in each of us.

The questions of the divinity of Jesus and the equality of the Holy Spirit to the other two members of the Trinity of God's presence, power, and creativity raged in the Church in its early centuries. Councils of the Church[27] argued the dogmas surrounding these two concepts against all extremes: Some said that Jesus was only human, others that Jesus was only divine. Some insisted that the Holy Spirit was equal to God; others declared that the Holy Spirit was simply an agent of God. As benign, even boring, as those issues may seem now, they divided the Church into ugly factions then. They were the questions of the age. And by the fourth century, they were finally settled definitively. Jesus was divine, the Spirit was a coequal part of the Trinity, Creator-Redeemer-Sanctifier were specific aspects of the saving work of God. Now, it was clear. We understood it. We agreed. At least theoretically.

Living out the implications of what we say we accepted, however, has been difficult, deficient, and often downright perverse. God was pure mystery, the Church argued, and then set out to define the cosmos, creation, and the afterlife with a kind of precision at least audacious if not embarrassing. When human understanding of the cosmos changed and creation began to look like evolution, it took years, centuries, for the Church to accept the fact that the Holy Spirit was speaking in languages not theological.

Jesus was born of a woman under the impulse of the Holy Spirit, the documents said, and then proceeded to ignore women in the plan of the Church entirely. When, after centuries of denial, the world began finally to realize that the female brain showed the same composition as the male brain, that the other half of the life force was in them, too, that a little girl could run as fast as a boy, that women could lead and manage and speak and write as well as any man, the Church insisted nevertheless that women had a "special nature" and a role more biological than spiritual.

God's Holy Spirit hovered over the waters in the process of Creation, the Church itself taught, and gave charisms, gifts, to the entire community—both sons and daughters— as the prophet Joel envisioned and the apostle Paul preached. Clearly, the Holy Spirit was speaking through females as well as males, but to what end? Spirit and charism and creation notwithstanding, the Christian community metamorphosed into a clerical system to such a degree that the gifts of the laity were locked out of synods and council chambers, chanceries and sacred studies, forever. The Holy Spirit speaks in tongues both lay and clerical, but no one listens to language that is lay. As a result, Pentecost is the feast that never really comes and confirmation is the sacrament that doesn't really count.

The Holy Spirit, we are told, is the spirit of Wisdom, of the feminine Sophia, in the Church. Each of us, we argue theologically, has a piece of that Wisdom, the Spirit working in us to build the people of God, the reign of God, the assembly of God on earth. But how can we do that when all the wisdom the Spirit has to offer never gets taken into account?

If we are to understand emerging consciousness as a manifestation of the Spirit of God alive in the land, then never has an age seen revelation, consciousness, and wisdom working more clearly than in this one. The signs of new awareness of the human relationship to God are everywhere, in all nations, in all peoples. The Holy Spirit has spoken through married couples and professional personnel about birth control, for instance. The Holy Spirit has spoken through women—and other eminent theologians, theological societies and male Scripture scholars, as well— about the ordination of women. The Holy Spirit has spoken through laity and bishops and multiple other rites of the Church alike about the ordination of married men. But no one listens. The Holy Spirit in people of good will is a voice crying in the wilderness, rejected, ignored, and reviled. One element of the Church determines the voice of the Spirit and does so, it seems, by refusing to listen to its other manifestations.

The question for this age, then, is not "'What' is the Holy Spirit?" as it was in centuries past. Our question is: "'Who' is the Holy Spirit?" How is it that only one part of the Church seems to qualify as voice, as wisdom, as last word on every word. The question is a defining one. Four hundred years ago, the Holy Spirit spoke through Martin Luther and all the reformers about the selling of relics, the inadequacy of merit theology, and clericalism. But it took three separate councils of the Church, hundreds of years apart, before the Church acknowledged the truth of those concerns. The Holy Spirit has a serious problem here.

God the Creator and Jesus the Way—always with us on the one hand, but never with us on the other—would move humanity, the early Church was now sure, by means of the promptings and presence of the Spirit of God who created us and who lives among us and is in us still. Holy Spirit was not a disembodied ghost, not an immaterial being. On the contrary. The Spirit embodied the life force of the universe, the power of God, the animating energy present in all things and captured by none. Because of the Spirit, Jesus was not gone and God was not distant, and the life force around us bore it proof. The Spirit was the restless urge to life in us leading life on to its ultimate.

The Spirit of God moves us to new heights of understanding, to new types of witness, to new dimensions of life needed in the here and now. The static dies under the impulse of the Spirit of a creating God. We do not live in the past. We are not blind beggars on a dark road groping our separate ways toward God. There is a magnet in each of us, a gift for God, that repels deceit and impels us toward good. The gifts are mutual, mitered to fit into one another for strength and surety.

We are, in other words, in the most refreshingly trite, most obviously astounding way, all in this together—equally adult, equally full members, equally responsible for the Church. Nor does any one dimension of the Church, then, have a monopoly on insight, on grace, on the promptings of God in this place at this time. The Spirit of God is a wild thing, breathing where it will, moving as it pleases, settling on women and men alike.

It is Wisdom, Sophia, that the world seeks, not "change," even when change becomes the only wise course. Change is a mechanical process that turns one thing into another regardless of its value, careless of its results. Wisdom, on the other hand, is a project of the soul. Wisdom sees through gloss and beyond difficulty to meaning and purpose and quality. Wisdom takes us to the eternal in time and makes time pregnant with promise. Because of Wisdom, dark becomes light and rough becomes possible. Wisdom brings the laser of truth to bear on both the stone and straw of life, of both the humdrum and the complacently sophisticated of every ilk, sacred as well as secular.

The Holy Spirit stays with the Church to guide it, the tradition says. But in that case, we as institution and we as individuals alike must be open to that guidance, no matter the direction from which it comes. Even when it comes from science. Even when it comes from the laity. Even when it comes from women. Unless, of course, we want to argue that the Church belongs to clerics alone, in which case the theology of the Holy Spirit upon which the authenticity and present inspiration of the Church depends, shrivels and dies. The thought of it curdles the soul a bit.

To be a woman and read Wisdom literature—the meanderings of the spiritual mind through the dregs and the divine of the human condition—is especially difficult. There Wisdom is woman, but women have no part in its development. Here, the Spirit that is called "Holy Wisdom," "Sophia," is also called "she." Scripture calls the Spirit *ruah*, a feminine word, to describe the feminine aspect of the Godhead, the breath of God, the mighty wind that hovered over the empty waters at the beginning of life in the process of Creation—all feminine images of a birthing, mothering God, of pregnant waiting and waters breaking and life coming forth. But when Wisdom declares itself, it is always through a male message, without a woman in sight. And so the Wisdom limps.

This Spirit, this living Wisdom that is God, lifts us above ourselves, tunes us to the voice of the Creator around us and within us, comes upon us with gentle force or terrible consciousness, and cares for life, day in, day out, unrelenting in its urge for wholeness. The Spirit prods us, proves us, brings life in us to creative fullness. The Spirit is God with us, in us, around us, breathing us to life. And yet, having defined the Spirit as Wisdom, as *ruah*, as "she," this feminine force of life as feminine is promptly submerged, totally forgotten, completely ignored. The masculine images reappear, the genderless God is gendered, and the fullness of

God, the fullness of life, is denied in the Church. The Church itself stays half whole. And the Spirit ceases to breathe in it more than half.

Indeed, we are born Christian but spend our lives learning what that means. We get confirmed and pledge ourselves to defend the faith but learn only later that faith is something that grows from one life revelation to another. Each stage takes courage, takes faith, takes openness to the Spirit. We have no problem whatsoever believing that God created us and that Jesus leads us; but when we really believe that the Spirit is in each of us showing us, as a church, the way, courage is needed and faith is taxed. The Spirit is bigger than the institution. The Spirit lives in us, driving us on and demanding a response from each of us and all of us for the sake of creation, for the sake of the Church itself.

When we pray, "I believe in the Holy Spirit..." we pray a prayer we have yet to see completed. We pray a prayer the fulfillment of which the Church denies to most of us. The learning is embryonic. The insights are fractional. Confirmation is a sacrament still in process and still in danger of being aborted—at least for half the human race and most of the laity as well.

23

THE HOLY CATHOLIC CHURCH...

Perhaps the reason I remember both situations so well is because I have been struggling with the implications of each of them ever since. They present, in fact, the central questions, the basic questions, for anyone who becomes embroiled in the struggle between truth and authority, between faith and institution, between catholic and Catholic. The interesting thing is that I do not remember the specific incidents that prompted either remark. All I know now is that in my mind it was some then-recent Church directive bringing all the ecclesiastical imperial power of Rome to bear on one more issue as soul-shattering as habits for nuns, the use of feminine pronouns in Church documents, the ranking of eucharistic ministers, or the right to discuss the ordination of women and married men. One thing I do remember clearly, however, is that disappointment, disillusionment, and a kind of weary dismay consumed me at the thought of it.

For the sake of my own spiritual accountability, I had to make someone in the institution understand the anger and the damage that these kinds of things were doing to the faith and to the Church. So, in a car coming into Washington from the airport I poured it all out. He and I had been friends for years. He was a priest now, a member of a religious order, a sensible, pastoral, mature, and free-spirited man who had little time for theory in life and took on the present, callow and bare, one day at a time. The gospel came first, he always said, and everything else was secondary. If anyone could hear the seriousness of the situation, could provide some light, could give some support, it was surely he.

I was not prepared for the response. Instead of hearing out the frustration in my voice, instead of counseling how to promote the concern with as much care for the health of the Church as well as the urgency of the question, he simply dismissed my whole disquiet with a short, impatient shrug of his shoulders and toss of his hand. "Ah, just ignore them," he said with an exasperated frown. "Why do you give them so much power over you? Who cares what they say? That system is all over. It's only a matter of time. Just forget them." Easy for you to say, I thought. Women live under the rules that the men who "forget" them are pleased to make. The number of women whose lives would be curtailed, whose vocations would be lost, whose gifts would be ignored by the Church while the male world "just forgot them," and—worse—did nothing of conscience to challenge their own systems, made me a little ill.

I dropped the conversation and moved on to the kind of superficial comments that cover up the dangerous topics we can't negotiate in life, but the questions with which the abrupt dismissal of the subject left me were worse than the ones I'd brought to it in the first place. What kind of church was this? Who were these Christians? How was it that living the gospel always seemed to become conflated with maintaining the institution when new questions challenged old answers? Unity, they insisted, preempted every other consideration, whatever its cost in people. In other words, when in doubt, say nothing. When in disagreement, pretend not to notice. When inspired by concerns beyond the merely institutional, ignore the annoyances that bring the gospel to test in our time. So much for the stirrings of the Holy Spirit. So much for the needs of the laity. So much for the sacramental system in a church which, when faced with a choice between sacraments and maleness, chose always for maleness. How, I wondered then, and wonder still, can we cavalierly forget what the institution does in the name of the Church?

The second incident was no less unsettling. This time it was a woman who had, indeed, opted to forget them. "Why would any self-respecting woman stay in that institution?" she asked me pointedly. She had long ago ended any kind of church affiliation. "This institution is dangerous to women and other living things," she said after trying for years to raise the woman's question in the local parish. "How can you accept that kind of human diminishment and believe in that church? Aren't you just cooperating in perpetuating a sinful system? Aren't you just trying to put a good face on a bad thing? If you stay in something like that, aren't you complicit in the sin?" The questions smack of the kind of morality I myself had wanted from the priest. Why didn't I "do" something?

As the years have gone by, I have come to the conclusion that they were both right, both of them have a piece of hard wisdom to share. To survive a basically good institution in the throes of creeping change, we have to forget one kind of church and recommit ourselves to the creation of the other one, the one created by the Holy Spirit, rather than the one created by centuries of political accretions and clerical control.

It is not that the clergy and the papacy are not the Church. They are, of course. But what has really been forgotten, both by us and by them, is that they are not the whole Church. They are not the model of the Church that sprang up in Jerusalem after the death of Jesus, formed by women in house assemblies, preached by laymen on street corners in Greece, witnessed in the whole Christian community of Jews who saw the gifts of the Holy Spirit—prophecy and tongues, discernment of spirits and healing, service and proclamation—in one another.

To say "I believe in the holy catholic church" is to believe in a church beyond the walls of catholic ghettoes, above the authority of any one man, steeped in the Christ-life and the treasure house of holiness common to the whole band of believers from Pentecost to now. The church is not the Church. The church is at most the point at which people come to become the Church. Together. The Church is the gathering of the seekers who celebrate the continuing presence of Christ among them, in them, and through them. The Church is the assembly of believers who are sign of the Christian tradition, who make Jesus present now, who by serving, loving, proclaiming, and witnessing to the Jesus in whom they believe make the link between the human community and the touch of God in time. Why and how could we possibly think otherwise? The reasons are more political than theological.

A church defending itself against political pressures from without and theological challenges from within tended, over the centuries, to forget its charismatic nature. Governments threatened to consume a church that had itself become an imperial power. Theological differences threatened to undermine the credibility of the tradition beyond recognition. Maintaining the institution itself became the key project of the institution. It touched us all. To grow up Irish in English Boston, to be a Catholic in a white Anglo-Saxon Protestant country formed fierce defenders of the "faith," meaning uncritical conservators of the parish, the pope, and the parish priest. The effects of such a mentality do the Church itself no good whatsoever.

The "church" became too often reduced to mere symbols of itself: its chanceries and seminaries, its parishes and clergy, its identification with some kind of Roman superstructure, its body of laws and privileges, holdings, dogmas and decrees. All operating outside, above, and beyond the assembly of the faithful, the gathering of the believers who were its body. Now down was up and up was down. The people came to exist for the Church, rather than the Church for the service of Christ in the breathing, believing community. "The Church teaches....The Church instructs....The Church says....The Church requires...," all commonplaces of the institution, became more important directives, more standard explanations, than "The gospel tells us....The gospel shows us...or Jesus says." The "church" had become a freestanding enterprise, a Roman corporation, a place to which people went to receive sacraments more done to them than accomplished in them, an ecclesiastical site rather than the gathering of a witnessing people themselves. It was a church inveighed, an institution in threat for its life.

This Church guards itself from the theological incompetence of a laity too ill-prepared to understand the niceties of theology—despite the fact that every church document written brings potential judgment on their lives, functions in secret—rather than in the heart of the assembly, and too often operates out of past answers rather than face present questions. But that is not the church the Creed asks us to profess.

The Creed calls us to believe in a church that is "holy" and "catholic," a church that is a promise of the Christ-life, a guarantee of universal acceptance. A church that is "holy" does not profess to be perfect. Perfection is a myth of human imagination that refuses to allow Being to be in us. Perfection sets out to control the world; holiness sets out to be a blessing to it. When law rules, holiness is impossible because law sets a false ceiling on life. To be law-bound is to assume that we know what God expects in every situation and, more than that, that what we want, God wants. When withdrawal dictates our responses to the world, when what we seek is freedom from human contamination rather than immersion in the great human struggle for wholeness, that is not holiness, that is not the willingness to take life on its own terms with Jesus as a model and God as our growth-point.

The Church must engage itself in the great questions of humankind. The Church, to be holy, must be Jesus with the lepers, Jesus with the women, Jesus beneath the cross that crucifies humanity. No amount of pomp, no amount of authority, no amount of prestige will substitute for a holiness made of the miracles of dailiness.

The Church is holy because it makes holiness its reason for existence. It beckons the human race to more than humanness. It reveals the holiness, the goodness, the God-embodiment of life by sacramentalizing it at every step: at birth, at death, in the midst of brokenness, in times of fear, at the core of human relationships, in the emptiness of soul that strikes every sincere seeker along the way, in the hunger of the human heart for wholeness. Everywhere, in life's simplest elements—water, oil, candles, music, community, bread, wine, incense—the Church exists to remind us of the sacredness of life, to point us to its fullness. In its sacraments, the Christian assembly celebrates the inbreaking of the sacred into the mundane, makes festival of the normal, finds God in the clay of life.

The Creed calls us to be a catholic church—a congregation of believers who embrace the world and everyone who walks it. The church that despises women, rejects homosexuals, demeans believers who hear the voice of God in another key or organizes itself into a sanctuary for the sophisticated of the world is sectarian, not Christian; Catholic, not catholic. Churches like that are clubs, not Christian

assemblies of those who believe in the person, the procla-
mations of Christ.

It is that holiness, that catholicity, that church that keeps
me in this community of sinners trying to be saintly. It is
that church that is often in tension with a church more site
than community, more pomp than people. That open-hearted
church is often in sin but never in arrogance.

That's the church I can't just "forget." It is also the
church I cannot leave. The other Church, the church of laws
and social levels, of clerical control and institutional defen-
siveness is not the church to which I belong. The priest was
right: that is the church that deserves to be forgotten. The
woman was right, too: That's the church our souls must
leave so that the Church of Christ can rise again. In all of
us.

IN THE COMMUNION OF SAINTS...

My family was part of that era of poor Irish immigrants who handled the pain of expatriation by not speaking of what they knew they could never see again. They never told stories about leaving Ireland, they never described the land they'd lived on, they never mentioned names or places lost but not forgotten. Life, it seemed, started only with us. There were no pictures, no stories, no letters, no talk of home or family left behind. But they taught us all the old Irish songs and did the jig at family parties and named the area in which they lived "Donegal Hill." My most precious memories are of family wakes where someone went to the prie-dieu in front of the coffin every hour, but the action really went on in the kitchen where aunts and uncles regaled themselves with memories of a deceased who, in the process, was dead no more. "To live in hearts we leave behind is not to die," Thomas Campbell wrote.[28] The older I grew, the more I knew the truth of it. Inside me lives a veritable gallery of smiling, strong, and friendly ghosts who guide me as I go.

But not only the family honored its ghosts. In the monastery, a plaque hangs on the wall of the chapel corridor with the name engraved on it of every deceased member the community has had since its founding in 1856, none of them ever to be forgotten. The *Memento Mori*—"remember, that you must die"—walkway between two wings of the building has embedded in its pillars the headstones of the earliest sisters on whose shoulders this community stands. At evening prayer a sister's death anniversary has been remembered every day for the last 142 years. "You talk your history," a visitor told us once after several weeks of dinner conversation, "as if it were your present." Our best nights are those moments in which older members of the community begin to tell stories about sisters long gone and even older than they. The community memory of its eighty-year-olds reaches back to a world far previous to this one and then even farther than that in stories they repeat from the storytellers before them.

All across the world, plants and flowers, trees and flags, mementoes and framed photographs stand on quiet graves to mark that communion of life that one generation feels with another. Our souls stretch always forward, yes, but our hearts stretch always back. The chain of life never breaks, the shape of soul never strains beyond what formed us, what filled us with life in the first place.

When the Creed talks about the "communion of saints" there is not a family, a nation, a group alive that does not recognize the meaning of the bond. But the Creed is talking about much more than family, about a great deal more than ethnic identities, about far more than long-lasting gratitude and longstanding models of lives well lived. There are two concepts embedded in the Creed's concern for the "communion of saints." The emphasis we choose to give the idea depends on which translation of the original terms we use.

To use the Greek version is to talk about those who share "a communion of holy things"—the Eucharist and all the other sacraments that implies.

Those who use the Hebrew translation of the term, on the other hand, concentrate on that communion of holy persons from whom we have inherited a faith strong enough, versatile enough, deep enough to shape our lives and direct our decisions. But, in reality, the two concepts are really one to those who understand that, at base, it is precisely our sense of family that governs the way we go about life, the things we value, the things we celebrate, the things for which we strive.

The Creed is talking, in other words, about the unity of strangers that forms around the image of the Christ who calls us always beyond our past into a demanding and sometimes lonely present. In communion with these people who have lived the faith to the end before us, we all trek on, alone but together, together but alone, depending on the hand and the sight of the other to take us further still. It is memory that calls us on.

Belief in the communion of saints is a call to immersion in the holy-making project of living out the life of Christ ourselves as so many have done before us. Strengthened by the model of the One "in whose memory" we make Eucharist—this thanksgiving for everything that is—we are bound to all it implies: We are bound to the reflective life that can lead us to great heights. We are bound to the unfinished work of bringing the world to the beatitudes. And we are bound, as well, to those who, in a special way, have modeled it before us and shown it to be worthwhile.

We talk a lot in the Western world today about a loss of values. In place of "Christendom," of religion, or creeds and canons, popes and imperial potentates, we have put only ourselves. Communal values have given way to personal priorities or private impulse. We have lost both the chastening gift of fear and the demanding gift of purpose. We have no time for hell, no notion of judgment, and no desire for sacrifice in a secular and highly individualistic culture. We do what pleases us in memory only of ourselves. The "communion of saints" is a concept well worth reviving, perhaps.

It is only in the social dimension of the "communion of saints" that sin, sacraments, and sanctity take on meaning. Without the idea of the communion of saints, even a life lived devoutly is nothing more than a personal excursion into spiritual narcissism. What is "sin" that does not rupture the bonds of human community. What kind of eucharist is it that does not bale us to the whole human race, make us present to it, and require our responsibility for its well-being?

The whole notion of "private" sin, that there is anything we can do that does not carry with it a public dimension, evaporates in the light of the "communion of saints." The sacraments are social acts. The healing of humanity belongs to us. The vocation to the development of the human condition belongs to us. The responsibility to bear a faith formative of the next generation belongs to us. The need to repent our rending of the human condition belongs to us. Then bombing the innocent becomes unthinkable, murdering to avenge murder becomes unacceptable, depriving children of food stamps becomes unconscionable. Then the communion of saints becomes real.

The Creed is not a call to believe in the Church. The Creed is a call to follow the Christ. Believing in a church that makes us feel holy ourselves by keeping in good repair a checklist of private devotions is easy. Believing in the Christ who demands that our sanctity be measured by our relationships to the rest of the human race is the real measure of the holy life. We have taken the word "community" and substituted the word "church" for it. The two are not synonyms, though certainly they ought to be. Interestingly enough, we know that without ever being told it, we touch that in the deepest part of the psyche without having to learn it. We realize at a very young age that it is our behavior in the human community, not our affiliation with a church, that will, in the end, measure the caliber of our lives.

We are bound to one another, each generation a link in the chain, each generation a standard for the one to come. The people over whose graves we weep are not simply people we have known or who, though strangers, have had the decency to disappear from an earth already overcrowded. No, we cry tears of loss only for those whose lives touched our own and made them better. We cry both for parents and for politicians, for friends and for public figures, for anyone who has lived out "the communion of saints," the Eucharist of humankind, the Christing of life and made it real in our own time, in our own neighborhoods, in our own world. We weep for those whose faith has formed our own.

The faith that brings us open-armed to one another is the faith that has the capacity to make us holy, not the faith we practice for our own benefit only. "The communion of saints" rests in the sacraments we share, in the sacramental lives we live for the sake of the world, in those who have passed them on to us shining and worthy, in those to whom we ourselves owe the same in times to come. If our values have changed in the Western world, if our aspirations have shifted for the worst in contemporary society, it may well be because we have lost this sense of the human character of the communion of saints and the communal dimension of the sacraments. In an attempt to do away with fancy and myth, to grow up beyond the fairy tales of faith, we may have left behind the bastions of our faith, our mentors and mainstays, as well. We have left our icons behind and gone facing into the wind with neither compass nor guide. We took the mythical Saint Christopher off the calendar in the interests of historical accuracy; we turned our heads away from women who defaced themselves to protect their virginity in recognition of the fact that sanctity had something to do with mental health and emotional balance. It was a proper posture to take. But to lose respect for the great lights along with the lesser ones, to forget Elizabeth of Hungary or Thomas More, Catherine of Siena or Martin of Tours, leaves us alone on the edges of life, lacking both models and guides.

When we turned away from tales of holy mutilation and spiritual neurosis, we failed to draw a distinction between the extreme and the brave, the balanced and the barely human characters whose legends grew layer upon layer in star-starved villages from age to age. Lacking heroes of substance and quality, we found ourselves instead in a world of drug-dealing rock stars and diet-crazed models.

One look around the Western world and it is clear that we have lost what people need most and will create out of nothing, if necessary: a sense of spiritual substance and holy sacrifice, long-suffering endurance and eternal fidelity. The very stuff of people like ourselves who have lived through the mundane and survived it, lived through tragedy and bettered it, lived through the immoral and righted it. We need a new sense of the saints before us, the saints around us, the saint within us, and the saints yet to come who will look to us for proof of the power of the holy.

The communion of saints calls us to keep an eye on the spiritual values of life so that we may live lives in which the material and spiritual are integrated, nourish each another, and give hope. Every culture has had its lesser gods. The purpose of the saints in each of them has been to remind the human community of wider vistas, to move the human experience to deeper roots, to draw the human heart to lasting treasures. Warning children of the immorality of rap stars, the hardheartedness of ruthless politicians, and the dangers of addictive behaviors without showing them another way reeks of the superficial. The Creed that calls us to believe in God is the same Creed that calls us to believe in ourselves, to honor the past, and to model a better future. It is when we substitute individualism, even a benign individualism, for the hard work of co-creation that we abandon the communion of saints.

It is precisely in the communion of saints that we find strength for the journey, hope in the face of despair, and sanctity whatever the sins to be transcended. It is here around the table together, in communion with the Christ who raised our eyes above the law to the God in whose service it is said to function, that we see the center of life raised on a cross, resurrected from the dead bones of past history, alive in the Spirit that makes bold the prophets of the age. Whatever we are facing has been faced before. Whatever we do will effect what is to come. Whatever Jesus is to people today has something to do with what we ourselves are today.

The communion of saints is the heritage we received, the promise we make to others, and strength for the journey in which we ourselves are engaged. It is eucharist, it is the sacramental life, flashed across the cosmos by the beam of my own life.

The communion of saints is not about the sinlessness of those who went before us. It is about sinfulness transcended, made holy in the milling of everyday life, of everyday politics, of everyday ecclesiastical consternation.

The communion of saints is every color, every level, every challenge of humankind. It is the cosmic vision of Christ made plain. It crosses time and culture and the quagmires of national politics and Church conflicts to leave us with a face of Church that is human, is us at our best. It is the Christ-face drawn differently in every age by every people.

To stand at an altar praying, "I believe...in the communion of saints" is to make a solemn promise to be what eucharist is all about: the life of Christ, the healing of humanity, the presence of the spirit of God, the willingness to sacrifice ourselves for the other. When we visit the graves and say the memorial prayers and tell the family stories over the bodies of the dead, we tell of the Christ we saw in them. We remember how it looked in them. We know in them what it is like to be driven by the consuming power of God, to be totally oriented toward God. The communion of saints stands before us, stark witness to the holiness of God, reminding us always to leave behind us for those yet to come a searing memory of the same.

THE FORGIVENESS
OF SIN...

The person telling the joke thought it was funny. To be polite, if nothing else, I managed one of those wan, anemic smiles that signal the mannered responses we make when we want to be kind but honest at the same time. In this case, what was supposed to be funny, I took to heart. "Jimmy, the local drunk, fornicator, embezzler, and philanderer dies," the storyteller spluttered, already laughing at the very thought of it. "His wife, a proper lady, wants a nice funeral for him to keep up appearances, if nothing else, so despite the fact that religion meant nothing to Jimmy, she goes to Father Muldowney, the parish priest. 'Please,' she begs the priest. 'I know that Jimmy was a scoundrel and never went to church, but can't you at least bury him and say a kind word over his body?' The priest looked at the poor pleading woman and felt sorry for her. 'Oh, all right,' the priest says, 'bring him to the church and I'll see what I can do.'

"The entire city and every one of his relatives down to his third cousins turned up at the funeral to hear what good a priest could possibly think of to say about a guy like this. Muldowney took a deep breath, looked out over the straining, expectant crowd, thought a minute, and said, 'I know Jimmy O'Brien was a drunk, a fornicator, an embezzler, and a philanderer. But next to the rest of his family, this guy was a saint.'" The storyteller moved away laughing too much to realize that I was not.

The fact of the matter is that I was too struck by the poignancy of the story to laugh at it. "Isn't it the truth?" I thought to myself. Next to me, everybody else on earth is a saint. To whose faults could I possibly point for exoneration of my own? Brokenness pervades the human condition, hides itself under the guise of perfectionism, makes us dissatisfied with ourselves and demanding of others. And yet the truth of it is so likely to elude us.

The situation is, in fact, a relatively common one. In one prominent New York City suburb, the story caused quite a stir: A known mafia chieftain, the headlines trumpeted, would be buried from the local Catholic church. People shook their heads in dismay. Many used the occasion to point out the hypocrisy of the Church. Self-congratulations on the virtue of our own private lives in comparison with his publicly sinful ones were everywhere. We read the headlines and clucked over the existence of organized crime but completely forgot about our own virtuous glee at the bombing of civilians or the evictions of the unemployed in this rich and righteous country. Nor did we ever stop to ask where all our wealth had come from while Third-World workers made our shoes, sewed our clothes, and picked our sugar cane for pennies a day. We clearly understood what it was to be illegal. We barely understood what it meant to be immoral.

Church history itself causes quite a stir, too: Sinful popes, errant clergy, and public sinners punctuate the movement of this "holy" church through time. Everywhere at every level sin lurks. But not so much as conscious, premeditated evil, perhaps, as it is careless, desperate, self-centered disregard for the rest of the human race, for the little people on whose shoulders we all stand, for the evil effects of our lives on the lives of others. It is just here, perhaps, where the Creed breaks into life with assurance and balm.

After calling our attention to the glories of creation, the infinite impact of Jesus and the Gospel in a highly rigid, crassly legalistic, ethnically closed world, and the continuing call of the Holy Spirit, the Creed ends with an admission of the rifts in the soul of humanity. It ends astounding for its gentleness. When it is all over—when there is no more life to barter for sport—we who have never completely bowed to the mind of God, the Creed says, never really become what we could have been, never noticed the damage we've done around us, always pled our innocence, our abuses, our misconstrued motives in this world, and never completely taken responsibility for anything, will be forgiven the crassness of our sins. Small, petty, selfish, mean, uncaring—and forgiven.

The most beautiful lines of the Creed, perhaps, have been reserved for the end of it. If there is a sign of the underlying authenticity of the Church—whatever it teaches, however it contradicts its own beliefs—this is surely it. This Church with all its legacy of guilt-making over the ages, all its own distortions of the human condition, believes passionately nevertheless in the forgiveness of sins.

The Creed does not talk about evil nor does it talk about guilt. It concentrates us only on the forgiveness of a Creator-God who, having made us, knows of what we are made. This God knows sincerity and values it over perfection. This God knows weakness and glories in bringing it to wholeness. This God does not make performance a criterion for love.

The implications of the statements are overwhelming. God forgives our spiritual deformities and private destructions, our pettiness and profoundly mean misconstructions of other people's motives, forgives our blindness and our denials. Indeed, we are a people cleft in the heart, but we do not own it. We are a people, one of whose greatest weaknesses is the inability to accept the weakness of others while we insist on the innocence of our own souls.

Perhaps forgiveness is the last thing mentioned in the Creed because it is the last thing learned in life. Perhaps none of us can understand the forgiveness of God until we ourselves have learned to forgive. Perhaps we cannot understand the goodness of God to us because we are so seldom that good to others. On the contrary, we want mercy for ourselves but exact justice for the remainder of humankind. God, on the other hand, the Creed implies, desires justice but gives mercy like a rushing river, gushes mercy like a running stream.

Forgiveness, perhaps the most divine of the divine attributes, ranks, as well, as the most basic of human processes, the one that really brings us to the zenith of ourselves. To forgive is to be like God. God the Forgiver stands before us, beckoning us to holiness, showing us forgiveness as the way to wholeness: to mental health, to personal growth, to independence of emotions, to freedom of soul. Among Jesus' last words on the cross are words of forgiveness. Jesus—come to the fullness of humanity, the end time, the final moment—goes burned into our mind as a forgiver. Clearly, to be everything we can become, we must learn to forgive.

But there are two kinds of forgiveness: one healthy, one not. One is of God, the other a kind of holy affectation, a game we play on ourselves in the name of holiness and wonder why it doesn't work. Forgiveness only works when we are as aware of what vengeance does to ourselves as we are of what it does to the other.

Forgiveness implies two options: We can forego the right to requital or we can simply choose to forego payment of a just debt. We can let go of resentment and the expectation of retribution or, in a gust of moral superiority, simply be generous enough to dismiss the obligation of the debtor. But not the debt. We cease to demand repayment but, down deep, we never forget that payment is still owed.

To forego repayment for harms done releases the debtor but continues to hold us captive to the uncompensated debt, continues to eat away at the inside of us forever. We keep the debtor in spiritual servitude and ourselves in hostile chains. If all we do is to accept the fact that there will be no repayment coming for the harm that was done to us and make the best of a bad thing, the debt remains. Always there, never satisfied. We ourselves are never free of it.

But the failure to forgive, the unyielding memory of the debt, is too great a burden to carry. It smothers the joy out of life. It blocks our own ability to move. It makes growth impossible. It traps us in the juices of the snake that bit us. That is not the mercy of the forgiving God who wipes out the past and, everyday, makes all things new again. To forego the need for requital releases us as well as our debtor from further harm. We free the debtor from shame and ourselves from bitterness.

And do not be misled. The Creed is clear about the situation. The Creed is talking about forgiveness for sin, real sin, not merely the invalidation of some kind of gross but basically benign misunderstanding. Harm has been done. Trust has been betrayed. Goodness has been foresworn for personal advantage. Someone has, like Cain, ceased to be my keeper and slain my heart. Then forgiveness, not dissembling, is imperative. This violation of ourselves is not about social formality. This is about relationships rent. This is about repair. This is about the need for real forgiveness, not cheap forgiveness, the kind counseled for the sake of a false peace. "Oh, don't let it bother you" is not an answer to sin. "Just don't pay any attention to it," does not erase the pain in the heart. "Just forget it. Put it down," dismisses both the sinner and the sinned-against. It asks for tawdry, cocktail-party forgiveness, for "niceness" that fails to diminish the pain, that leaves the sore raw but covered over by the cosmetics of civility waiting to erupt again. This is

not the kind of forgiveness that makes for peace, either between people or between nations.

Real forgiveness relies, like the forgiveness of God, on
full acknowledgment of the act that impaled the heart of a
person, full knowledge of the motive, full acceptance of the
human condition: People do these things. It is not so much
what a person does to us that is the essence of forgiveness.
It is what we do because of the sorrow we suffer that counts.

Premature forgiveness doesn't work. All it does is to
substitute formality where genuine connection should be. It
leaves the process of forgiveness incomplete. It risks the
possibility of submerging feelings that will only rise again
in us, displaced perhaps but there nevertheless, until we
embrace them, face them, and, perhaps still smarting from
the blow of them, move on beyond what cannot be changed
to another point in life. Then, all the ruptures can be re-
paired and forgiveness can be total because the fruits of sin
have finally come to full. Not because they were good but
because we went beyond them. That is divine forgiveness,
the awareness that though evil has been done, the spirit is
whole.

This prayer found by the side of a dead child at a concentration camp at the end of World War II may tell it all:

O Lord,
    Remember not only the men
        and women of goodwill,
    But all those of ill will.
    But do not remember all the suffering
    They have inflicted upon us;
    Remember the fruits we have bought
    Thanks to this suffering—
    Our comradeship, our loyalty, our humility,
    Our courage, our generosity,
        the greatness of heart

Which has grown out of all of this;
And when they come to judgment,
Let all the fruits which we have borne
Be their forgiveness. Amen.

It is only when we forgive that peace comes. When we suppress the pain that comes from sin, when we seek retribution rather than a new beginning, then the evil of vengeance and the failure of forgetfulness reproduce evil in abundance, repeat evil everywhere.

The sufi, Imam Husayn, called the king of martyrs, said: "Nobility is to choose forgiveness when revenge is in your power."

It is easy to talk of perfection. It is commonplace to talk of union with God. It is simple to varnish over feelings with propriety. But to reach to the heights of the Creed, to believe in forgiveness and so to be forgiving, now that is difficult. Until we know what it is to forgive the other, to walk beyond the crush of hurt and live again, holding no grudges, requiring no retribution, seeking no compensation, to liberate the sinner from the weight of the sin, we can never understand the forgiveness of God. More, we may never ourselves put on the heart of God.

The Creed leaves us with the image of a God for whom forgiveness is of the essence and from whose love we are all bound to learn.

If anything proves the Godness of Jesus, if anything calls us to the divine in ourselves, if anything inspires belief, surely it is the words on the cross that beg forgiveness for the unforgivable. Now, for our own sake, as well as the sake of the rest of the world, it's our turn to forgive.

26

THE RESURRECTION OF THE BODY AND LIFE EVERLASTING.

The Fourth UN Conference on Women in Beijing was a veritable Eden of liberation. Here was the paradise where all oppression ceased, I thought. Here equality was a given, differences were respected, and opportunity was basic to the very structure of the community. Feminists, who by definition included everyone, healed the world, saw persons as persons, whatever their color, whatever their diversity. But, I learned, Beijing made things very clear: Feminists may hold a philosophy of openness, but achieving it in the structures in which they exist is another thing entirely. The problem is that few, if any of us, noticed.

One day, crowded into a pushing, shoving wave of wet and musty humanity on the way up the steps of the main conference hall on the mall, I realized that somehow or other I had gotten myself into the middle of a public demonstration reminiscent of other places, other times. There ahead of us, blocking the doors to the auditorium on a rainy day, Chinese mud slopping around our ankles, was a phalanx of wheelchairs. The chanting was loud and clear. These were handicapped women demanding access rights to lectures, all of which were scheduled for walk-up accommodations. Chinese organizers, not the forum leaders themselves, had determined the lecture sites; but none of us had noticed the situation. We didn't create the situation, but we were totally insensitive to it, nevertheless — or if not insensitive, at least acquiescent. I knew the problem. After all, I had lived in a wheelchair myself for a period in life. But until I saw the chairs, heard the chanting, saw the signs, read the handouts, it had never crossed my mind that there was an entire mass of people there whose bodies were being allowed to bridle their minds, diminish their life experiences, limit their social contacts, and, in the end, suppress their spirits. And they are everywhere.

In fact, we all forget. Why? Because of rampant selfishness in a pathologically individualistic world? Because of a kind of terminal self-centeredness? I doubt it. My fear is that it goes much deeper than that. The problem, I think, may be that we have come to think of our bodies as irrelevant to our selves because bodiliness has always been disparaged in Western culture. Bodies, we have long been taught, either directly or indirectly, were seeds of sin or barriers to spirituality. Bodies, we learn from TV ads and girlie magazines, from health club ads and clothing stores, must be perfect. But they are not. As a result, we have learned to hate our bodies or, if not that, at least to ignore them and if not that certainly, ironically, to confuse the body with the person. It is a problem of deep theological significance, not just for people whose challenges are physical, but for the rest of us, too. It effects our spirituality as much as it does our attitudes.

In my generation, philosophy courses were a standard part of a college education. Like every other graduate of the average liberal arts college, I had studied the conflicting theories of Platonic dualism—the independence of body and soul, the primacy of the spirit—and the "De Anima," Aristotle's treatise on the human soul, that argued for the integration of the two. I knew that the Platonists taught that the body was a prison for the soul, that the Gnostics considered the body evil and that the Aristotelian school integrated the two so tightly that the death of the body simply extinguished any hope for the life of the soul. Cultures such as these, therefore, had no time for the body. It was a prison to be escaped, simply a vehicle for reason, the genesis of evil. An old anthropology, a discarded world-view? Not completely and not necessarily.

The ugly head of negative asceticism aimed at the discipline of the body has shown itself again and again in history. As recently as the twentieth century itself, Jansenism has managed a fine grip on the seascape of the human psyche, the exercises of the spiritual life. "Spirituality," in these earlier understandings, required a person to reduce life to its spiritual dimensions alone. The separation of body and soul became a goal to be desired, a piety to be pursued. Manuals cautioned seriously "spiritual" people to beware anything that satisfied the senses—the smell of flowers, a surfeit of food—and to control the flesh at least simply, by living a life of personal sacrifice, or radically, by practices as extreme as self-flagellation. Even garden variety spirituality cautioned discipline, control, and moderation at all levels, the assumption being that delight at anything led to excesses in everything. The body became the focus, the arbiter, the nemesis of the spiritual life. The body, rather than the person, took center stage in the spiritual life.

Gone was the acuity of early Christian consciousness that the spirituality of the Christian devolved out of the need to build the New Age into the present reign of God. We had, by virtue of our concentration on control of the flesh, identified spirituality almost totally with the control of the body. And, in the process, we had managed to diminish the notion of person—that configuration of values, delights, abilities, and character—that make the human being more than body. We had, moreover, managed by this paranoid obsession with distinguishing matter from spirit, to miss the relationship between spirituality and corporeality, two aspects of the one person that we all are.

At the same time, I also knew—thanks to courses the value of which only became clearer as life went on—that biblical anthropology never thought of the body as separate from the soul. The Creator had created both, Jews reasoned, and would, therefore, redeem both. How that would happen, they could not agree. That it would happen, they were sure. Most of all, I knew that all of these schools of thought had affected the way my own society as well as theirs viewed life, as well as death.

If the purpose of life is to liberate the soul from the body, as Plato argued, then the body and all material things were at best useless. If the life of the soul depended on the life of the body, as Aristotle argued, then life was nothing more than a burst of painful consciousness on an infinitesimally small screen, without purpose, without hope. If body and soul were integrated, as Aquinas argued, and the soul, the Spirit in us, was of God, then the body was good and the person was more than the body. I "knew" all of those things but I didn't understand any of them until I met Mary Louise.

Mary Louise had been in a wheelchair since she was four years old. She had been born with muscular dystrophy, a disease that destroys the neurological fibers of human musculature and dooms a person to progressive paralysis. When I met her, she had a full body brace to go with the wheelchair in which she sat sixteen hours a day in order to keep her from slumping over in it, a pulp of uncontrollable flesh. She could bob her head a bit and use one thumb on one hand. But it was Mary Louise who really taught me what ancient Judaism and philosophical Greece had in mind when the Jews developed no word at all for "body," and the Greeks used two—*sarx* for flesh but *soma* for the self.

Mary Louise was not a body, she was a personality with great abilities, keen vision, and high ambitions. She got a college degree, began to travel to conventions at great physical effort, declared her sexuality, moved into a private apartment in an independence court, and danced in a wheelchair. Mary Louise taught me in living color that human beings are not torsos who cease to exist when the frame that shapes us fails to function at some level we set as normative, arbitrarily at times, unjustifiably often. We are persons. Stephen Hawking. Franklin Delano Roosevelt. Mary Louise. All of us. And, suddenly, the Creed took on new life. Then, the phrase "the resurrection of the body and life everlasting" began finally to make sense. I began to understand that resurrection is not about matter, it is about life. What we believe in when we say "I believe in the resurrection of the dead and life everlasting" is not the opening of graves and the revival of corpses. Resurrection in the Christian paradigm does not imply a return to earthly life. What we believe by resurrection is that life has a purpose and a quality that does not end at the grave. We believe that the God who created us does not create us to abandon us but brings us finally, somehow, home to the fullness of life. Resurrection is simply another part of the process of growing into God. "Life" as we know it, "time" as we chart it, are simply temporary points to an eternal journey in a universe of unlimited mystery, endless possibility.

But "resurrection" is not simply concerned with what we think about death. It has a great deal to do with what we think about life, as well. The notion that matter, bodies, things exist full of goodness, spun from glory, ripe with God, turns the world and everything in it into diamonds of revelation, stones off of which glance the light that is creation.

Then, everything holds up a mirror into eternity for us. Everything gives us one more secret about the nature, not only of creation, but of the Creator, as well. Then, everything is sacred.

In a culture that once taught the essential evil of matter, that now teaches the exploitation of matter and calls it progress, the "resurrection of the body" heralds the goodness of creation. It calls creation to honor itself in a culture that insults nature by virtue of its birthright. But as long as matter is holy, all of life is holy and nothing is here to be wantonly destroyed. The notion that creation exists for human beings is routinely misconstrued to mean that we have a right to the fruits of the earth, no holds barred, no limits measured, no consideration given, no respect required. The truth is, however, that though the entire rest of creation can exist without humanity, humanity cannot exist without creation. We do not have the right to destroy with impunity, to consume without conscience, to exploit without shame. We are a part of everything that is and it of us. We are one with a universe that will one day reclaim us.

The Creed's call to resurrection stretches our vision of life, gives us back to the glory in the silt of us, calls to life that is not corruptible. Death makes life possible, just one more season in the cycle of creation. Resurrection makes life worthwhile, the growing into God for which we were born and in which process we labor even now.

Life is good, not evil, the Creed teaches, but life is not all there is. Like an idea become a song, like a seed become a flower, like a match become a flame, we will someday come to a new kind of life, eternal in spirit and changed in form. And how can we be so sure of that? Because God has planted the proof all around us, if only we could see. It is, as a matter of fact, metamorphosis, change into otherness, that is the very nature of life. "Are we the same as God or different from God?" the disciple asked the ancient. "We are neither the same nor different," the master answered. "We are like the ocean and the wave. Not one. Not two." Life is a becoming into the fullness of the self that knows no boundaries, grows in form, lives in the spirit of the Spirit, and has no end.

27

AMEN.

"Those who have lived well for their own time have lived well for all times," the proverb teaches. The point is clear: Not only do we die into resurrection ourselves but if we have lived with respect for life, for the living, we leave resurrection in our wake as we go. The way we live ripples across time, touching people we never see, changing places we never went, singing a sound that never ends. To see the individual life as insignificant is to dismiss the meaning of life itself. As long as I live and breathe, who and what I am shakes the universe to its ankles. Good or ill, bright or bleak, glory or degradation follows each of us, marking our lives and determining our merits. What we think counts. What we do changes things. What we believe gives shape to the clay around us. To say "I believe" is to compose the universe according to my own designs. To say "I believe" brings into being a world of thought, the seeds of which determine the future.

The Creed, therefore, is not an index of dogmas, although it has often been presented as that. It is, more, a catalog of choices, an inventory of possibilities, a roster of visions. It is a guide to the kind of life that weathers millennia and stays fresh whatever decays, whatever changes around us. It is a call to a great "amen," the great "Yes" to life.

Life is gracious and gifting. Its value, its impact, its beauty depend only on the things we say "amen" to as we go. It is what we believe that sculpts and guides us. It is the quest for meaning that leads us to eternity now and the now of eternity.

At one level, the Creed, a bare and musty thing, seems sterile and useless, the remnant of a simpler age marked by more tolerance for lesser answers. But at another level, as the years go by, we begin to discover that the Creed has squirreled its way into our souls in ways far deeper than dogma, hiding concepts under a patina of stilted phrases too conventional to be noticed. Or if noticed, easily ignored, usually dismissed, often denied. The Creed says nothing of note, perhaps, until the day comes when we find ourselves grasping for the lifelines that once we had and now have lost. Then in search of credibility, we begin to realize, at least unconsciously, that the Creed carries them all. It is the Creed that takes us back to the questions, the values, the signposts that give direction to our lives.

We find that it is the Creed that begs us to believe in belief itself. On the days when we finally realize that in our graspings for prestige, power, wealth, and security, we have put our trust in empty gods, it is the Creed that sends us back looking for the things that make sense out of life, that gives us lights to steer by, and brings us home to the best in ourselves.

The Creed does not define God. The Creed posits God. The Creed confronts us with the concept of faith and requires us to face the fact that God is as good an answer as we have to anything. Faith itself, devoid of answers, brings us to the appreciation of mystery.

The Creed rejoices in the body of us, brings us to see divinity in humanity, shows us life beyond life in the mind of the God who made us, sustains us, and calls us into timelessness. Life, the Creed concludes, is good. All of it: body as well as soul, emotion as well as reason, earth as well as eternity. All life is one, this one simply prelude to a fullness beyond suffering to hope undaunted. To reduce that kind of belief to fancy and fairy tale, to the pseudo-scientific and the implausibly obscure makes sport of the kind of belief that forms hearts, shapes minds, and liberates the human soul to revel in the presence of God in time.

Clear in its consciousness of a personal God, the Creed is halting in its designation of this God who is life energy, eternal force, pure spirit. Wordless to describe a God without gender it reduces that God to maleness. It contradicts itself in the most mundane of ways by making metaphor— and making it prescriptive—where no metaphor belongs. It warps the meaning of God and leaves half the human race with nowhere to go to find itself in God. But the grappling stretches us, nevertheless. The Creed turns us away from God the Machine, God the Unconcerned, God the Remote to find the God whose person is present among us.

The Creed reminds us that there is within us a reservoir of strength come from a strength far beyond us. We learn here that life is much bigger than we are and God much bigger than life. And yet, we live in the vortex of the Eternal Force that has arranged all things for our good, provided all things for our welfare, shared a power with us that has no end. We learn in the Creed that "almighty" is a verb called life and that what does not happen outside of us can be transformed within us to the stuff of growth and good.

By reminding us that God is the "creator," the Creed gives us a glimpse of destiny and an assurance of well-being. The One who made us cares for us, we come to understand, as life becomes a series of losses survived and blessings come to light. We learn most of all, that to be human is to be creature—with all the other creatures on earth. Not superior, not independent, but only part of everything that is, all of which is sacred.

Awareness of heaven, of that life beyond life, calls us

away from fairy tale and fantasy to consider our place in the cosmos, to bow before its immensity, to grow up spiritually. Life is unlimited potential, not to be imagined in terms of spiritual lollipops and thrones. Life is about growing up to God.

The Creed, earthy in its concerns, immersed in humanity as well as in God, reminds us that the God who created heaven created the earth as well. Earth breathes the breath of God as well as we. The welfare of the earth is as precious to the God of life as is the welfare of human life alone. The implications of such a concept reverse our rules of the game. We are not justified, the Creed implies, in polluting the globe, thickening the waters, poisoning the land. The earth is God's, not ours. That is a principle of our belief and a clear guidance into the twenty-first century, if humans, that is, are to survive the twenty-first century.

Belief in Jesus Christ is belief in the presence of God, alive and challenging everything we are and do. It is the image of Jesus debating the Pharisees, breaking ethnic boundaries, refusing nationalistic prejudices, rejecting militarism, feeding the poor that calls our conscience to the bar of God. If such is God's care for humankind, how can we say we believe in God and do less for humanity ourselves?

Remembering the God whose relationship with Jesus was unique, The Creed gives us the heart to believe that our own relationships with God can also be special, intimate, real, particular. But the links are too clear to be ignored: For us to be what Jesus was to God requires being what Jesus was to the world. We must carry the same spirit, feel with the same heart, see with the same eyes as the One who saw what God saw and gave his life for it.

The Creed puts before our eyes a model of authority that does not "lord it over us." It recalls for us the reign of God for which we seek—power for the powerless and justice rooted in mercy—and, in that simple image, creates for us a criterion by which to measure our own use of place, prestige and position. Here, the Creed teaches, is the lordship that is servanthood. This, the Creed says, is the only kind of authority to which we must give our allegiance. Whatever bullies and beats on the little ones, whatever takes by force or rules by fear is not of God. Jesus, the Lord, lords over nothing. Nor may those who pretend to govern in his stead.

The Creed brings us to recognize head-on the presence of the holy in life, the power of the unexplained and the reality of the unexplainable. The breath of God conceives in us all, one way or another, provided we are open to the impulse, provided we are sensitive to the voice. The unusual, the unexpected in life all birth the opportunity for holiness. It is up to us to embrace it.

Human life, modeled in Jesus, the Creed implies, carries within it the potential for divine duty, for full spiritual development, for growing into God. The humanity of Jesus is the hallmark of our own and the Creed, in confirming the birth of Christ, confirms its glory for us all.

In a church that makes sex the centerpiece of morality and women the sex that's defined by it, the Creed calls us to remember that women do not figure in the plan of God because they are sex objects but because they are cooperating agents, full adults, in the bringing of the will of God to humankind. In the Creed God enlists Mary as a decision-making member of the human race, not as pawn or a passive instrument of male designs. The Creed models for the Church the full participation of women, however slow the coming.

The Creed redeems suffering simply by regarding it as despicable. The Creed does not glorify masochism. The Creed does not justify oppression. It names it so that we can see its distorting impact, its cry to God for justice.

The emphasis on the responsibility of the individual in

the plan of God becomes starkest of all in the Creed. Because of one individual, Mary, God's presence comes into the world in a special way. Because of the actions of another individual, Pilate, God's glory in the human condition dies brutalized. None of us, the Creed implies, dares to forgive ourselves our own role in the coming of the reign of God.

When we refuse to confront evil, we crucify the good. The Creed is uncompromising about the effects of systems on the poor of the world, the disenfranchised of the world, the powerless of the world. Crucifixions abound when there is no one to speak for the voiceless, no one to wait at the foot of the cross, no one to call for the release of Jesus, the innocent one, rather than for the liberation of evil in our midst. Systemic sin, the weapon of organizations who discount the needs of the people for the advantage of the structures which support their ends, grinds people up, crucifies them everywhere. It uses people for systems and calls them militarily "collateral damage" or economically "unemployment statistics" or socially "the underclass." It tramples on the many for the profit of the few. Nothing shows us more clearly what the profits are about than the Creed and the Christ.

Jesus, the Christ, glorified, is remembered in the Creed as Jesus wanted to be remembered—as one of us. The Creed takes us to the grave of Jesus and lets us see our own. Confronted with death we are able to live life with more meaning, with more purpose. The Jesus whose death became life for many brings us to think beyond the grave, to understand the reason we were born in the first place.

Routine now for all its regularity, all its sclerosis of language, the Creed is really meant to be a thunderclap of awareness. There was a moment in time—a third day—after which nothing else was ever again quite the same. The Creed is a call to celebrate that day in our own lives, to become new again in our attitudes, fresh in our insights, pristine in our values. We are called to see again who this Jesus is for us and to respond.

Whatever the storms in life, the Creed causes us to think in its commitment to Ascension that there is another dimension, a mystical dimension, of life that brings us to see beyond and above the mundane to where life is really Life. The concept of Ascension leaves us with an awareness of the unfinishedness of creation and our role in its coming.

At the heart of the Creed is hope, the consciousness that Jesus did not live in vain, nor we as well. The Jesus who was crucified lives in us yet, requiring us to look to the time when the reign of God will be complete and Jesus plain to be seen in the fullness of creation. The world waits again for the One who will bring it fully to God and bring the reign of God fully to life in us. We wait, then, in anticipation but in awareness of the measure under which we work.

Every segment of the Creed brings us back to what we must be about if the Creed is, in the end, to be totally true. The thought of eternal justice, of final accountability for our part in the development of the humanity of the human race, of the dignity of individual decisions is a sobering one. It is also the cry of the Creed for us to realize that we must be about more than ourselves in life.

But the Creed does not orphan us. Conscious of the breath of God within us and around us, we can with confidence set out on the road to God knowing that it may be rocky but that it is at the same time well lit, brightly marked, wholly traversable because the Holy Spirit makes the path with us. We have not been left alone. Under the impulse of the Spirit, we go guided and safe.

However sectarian the world, the Creed calls us, in its truest interpretation, to more ecumenical perspectives. The truth is that we pray the prayers of the Creed in the heart of the Church, in the heart of God, in the heart of the search-

ing community. Nothing and no one is to be closed out.
Our God is not the God of the Catholic Church. Our God
is the God of the universe. Our creed is not denominational,
ethnic, racial, sectarian; it is cosmic.

Imbedded in the core of the Creed is the proof of its
value, its availability, its truth: It has been the faith of many,
the proving stone of life for generations before us, the high-
water mark for those to come. In communion with those
whose lives were tested against it and came to holiness because of it, we can with confidence go the same way with
models to guide us and weakness as our sign that our God
does not abandon us to a fate too difficult for us to bear
and a darkness too deep for us to fathom.

And most kindly of all, the Creed reminds us of our
frailty and promises our forgiveness. The Creed does not
call us to be perfectly sinless; it calls us to be perfectly trust-
ing that, if we try, the God who desires us will deliver us
beyond ourselves.

For those for whom belief is the ground of meaning and
the foundation of purpose, the Creed is memory and guide.
Then, an ancient creed becomes new again. Then, life speaks
to the heart with new timbre for a new age:

> I believe in one God
> who made us all
> and whose divinity infuses all of life
> with the sacred.

> I believe in the multiple revelations
> of that God
> alive in every human heart,
> expressed in every culture,
> and found in all the wisdoms
> of the world.

I believe
that Jesus Christ,
the unique son of God,
is the face of God
on earth
in whom we see best
the divine justice,
divine mercy,
and divine compassion
to which we are all called.

I believe in the Christ
who is One in being with the Creator
and who shows us the presence of God
in everything that is
and calls out the sacred in ourselves.

I believe in Jesus, the Christ,
who leads us to the fullness
    of human stature,
to what we were meant to become
before all time
and for all other things that were made.

Through Christ
we become new people,
called beyond the consequences
    of our brokenness
and lifted to the fullness of life.

By the power of the Holy Spirit
he was born of the woman Mary,
pure in soul
and single-hearted—
a sign to the ages
of the exalted place
of womankind

in the divine plan
of human salvation.

He grew as we grow
through all the stages of life.
He lived as we live
prey to the pressures of evil
and intent on the good.
He broke no bonds with the world
to which he was bound,
He sinned not.
He never strayed from the mind of God.
He showed us the Way,
lived it for us,
suffered from it,
and died because of it
so that we might live
with new heart,
new mind,
and new strength
despite all the death
to which we are daily subjected.

For our sake
and for the sake of eternal Truth
he was hounded
harassed
and executed
by those
who were their own gods
and who valued the sacred
in no other.

He suffered so that we might realize
that the spirit in us
can never be killed

whatever price we have to pay
for staying true to the mind of God.

He died
but did not die
because he lives in us
still.

"On the third day" in the tomb
he rose again
in those he left behind
and in each of us as well
to live in hearts
that will not succumb
to the enemies of life.

He changed all of life
for all of us thereafter.
He ascended into the life of God
and waits there
for our own ascension
to the life beyond life.

He waits there,
judging what has gone before
and what is yet to come
against unending values
and, in behalf of eternal virtue,
for the time when all of life
will be gathered into God,
full of life and light,
steeped in truth.

I believe in the Holy Spirit,
the breath of God
on earth,
who keeps the Christ vision present

to souls yet in darkness,
gives life
even to hearts now blind.
Infuses energy
into spirits yet weary, isolated,
searching and confused.

The spirit has spoken
to the human heart
through the prophets
and gives new meaning
to the Word
throughout time.

I believe in one
holy and universal church.
Bound together by the holiness of creation
and the holiness of hearts forever true.

I acknowledge the need
to be freed from the compulsions
of my disordered life
and my need for forgiveness
in face of frailty.

I look for life eternal
in ways I cannot dream
and trust
that creation goes on creating
in this world
and in us
forever.

Amen.

Amen to creation, to the God who is life, to courage, to hope, to the spirit of truth, to nature, to happiness, to wholeness, to the place of women in the plan of God, to the Christ who calls us beyond the boundaries of ourselves, to forgiveness, to everything that makes living the first step in the stretching of the heart to the dimensions of God. Amen. Amen. Amen. In all of this we can surely believe. As God has.

NOTES

1. Bernard L. Marthaler, *The Creed* (Mystic, CN: Twenty-Third Publications, 1987) 3.
2. Anthony Kenny, ed., *Oxford History of Philosophy* (Oxford: Oxford University Press, 1994) 4–12.
3. Marthaler, vii.
4. Jack Miles, *God* (New York: Alfred A. Knopf, 1995) 262.
5. Elizabeth Rankin Geitz, *Gender and the Nicene Creed* (Harrisburg, PA: Morehouse Publishing, 1995) 15–16.
6. Geitz, 17.
7. Gerald O'Collins, S.J., and Mary Venturini, *Believing and Understanding the Creed* (New York: Paulist, 1991) 25; Geitz, 15.
8. Kenny, 55–80.
9. "Pope Edges Closer to Evolution Theory-Human Origins News," *MSNBC Staff and Wire Reports*, Wednesday, October 23, 1996.
10. Francis Bacon, "The Great Instauration" (1620) *Works*, Vol. 4, p. 20, Carolyn Merchant, *The Death of Nature: Women, Ecology and the Scientific Revolution* (San Francisco: Harper Collins, 1983) 17.
11. Andrew Wilson, ed., *World Scripture: A Comparative Anthology of Sacred Texts* (New York: Paragon House, 1991) 85.
12. R.C.D. Jasper and G.J. Cuming, eds., *Prayers of the Eucharist: Early and Reformed* (New York: Oxford University Press, 1980) 23, as cited in Geitz, 43.
13. *The Diary of Søren Kierkegaard*, Pt. 5, Sect. 4, #136 (ed. by Pete Rohde, 1960) 1843 entry.
14. Karl Rahner, *Sacramentum Mundi: An Encyclopedia of Theology*, Vol. 1 (New York: Herder and Herder, 1969) 169–170; Marthaler, 67–69.
15. Pamela Schaeffer, "Woman Cuts Into Liturgy, Asks to Be Priest," *National Catholic Reporter* 6 February, 1998: 5.
16. Marthaler, 123.
17. Rahner, Vol.3, 380.
18. Rahner, Vol. 3, 380.
19. Marthaler, 152.

20. John Donne, "Devotions Upon Emergent Occasions," Meditation 17 (1624).
21. Marthaler, 169–172.
22. Marthaler, 167.
23. Marthaler, 198.
24. Marthaler, 184.
25. Raymond Brown, Joseph A. Fitzmyer, and Roland E. Murphy, eds., *Jerome Biblical Commentary* Vol. 2 (Englewood Cliffs, NJ: Prentice-Hall, Inc., 1968) 168.
26. Christopher Frye, "A Sleep of Prisoners" in *Three Plays* (New York: Oxford University Press, 1960) 209.
27. Marthaler, 248–252.
28. Thomas Campbell, *Hallowed Ground,* 1744.

BIBLIOGRAPHY

Bass, Dorothy C., ed., *Practicing Our Faith*. San Francisco: Jossey-Bass, 1997.

Børresen, Kari Elisabeth, ed., *The Image of God: Gender Models in Judaeo-Christian Tradition*. Minneapolis, MN: Fortress, 1995.

Carmody, John Tully, and Denise Lardner Carmody. *Christian Uniqueness and Catholic Spirituality*. New York: Paulist, 1990.

Claudel, Paul. *I Believe in God: A Meditation on the Apostles' Creed*. Translated by Helen Weaver. New York: Holt, Rinehart and Winston, 1963.

Congar, Yves. *I Believe in the Holy Spirit*. Trans. David Smith. New York: Crossroad Herder, 1997.

Coward, Harold, ed., *Life after Death in World Religions*. Maryknoll, NY: Orbis, 1997.

Easwaran, Eknath. *Thousand Names of Vishnu*. Petaluma, CA: Nilgiri Press, 1987.

Geitz, Elizabeth Rankin. *Gender and the Nicene Creed*. Harrisburg, PA: Morehouse Publishing, 1995.

Grey, Mary C. *Prophecy and Mysticism: The Heart of the Postmodern Church*. Edinboro: T&T Clark, 1997.

Howard-Brook, Wes. *John's Gospel & The Renewal of the Church*. Maryknoll, NY: Orbis, 1997.

Jasper, R.C.D., and G.J. Cumming, eds., *Prayers of the Eucharist: Early & Reformed*. New York: Oxford University Press, 1980.

Johnson, Elizabeth A. *She Who Is: The Mystery of God in Feminist Theological Discourse*. New York: The Crossroad Publishing Company, 1992.

Kenny, Anthony, ed. *Oxford History of Western Philosophy*. Oxford University Press, 1994.

Knitter, Paul F. *One Earth Many Religions: Multifaith Dialogue and Global Responsibility*. Maryknoll, NY: Orbis, 1996.

_____ *Jesus and the Other Names: Christian Mission and Global Responsibility*. Maryknoll, NY: Orbis, 1996.

Knox, Ronald. *The Creed in Slow Motion*. New York: Sheed and Ward, 1949.

Küng, Hans. *On Being a Christian*. Trans. Edward Quinn. Garden City, NY: Doubleday & Company, 1976.

_____ *Eternal Life? Life After Death as a Medical, Philosophical, and Theological Problem*. Trans. Edward Quinn. Garden City, NY: Doubleday & Company, 1984.

_____ *Global Responsibility: In Search of a New World Ethic*. New York: Crossroad, 1991.

_____ *Credo: The Apostles' Creed Explained for Today*. Trans. John Bowden. New York: Doubleday, 1993.

LaCugna, Catherine Mowry, ed., *Freeing Theology: The Essentials of Theology in Feminist Perspective*. HarperSanFrancisco, 1993.

Lash, Nicholas. *Believing Three Ways in One God: A Reading of the Apostles' Creed*. Notre Dame: University of Notre Dame Press, 1992.

Loades, Ann. *Spiritual Classics from the Late Twentieth Century*. London: Church House Publishing, 1995.

Macquarrie, John. *Principles of Christian Theology*. New York: Charles Scribner's Sons, 1966.

Marthaler, Bernard L. *The Creed*. Mystic, CN: Twenty-Third Publications, 1987.

McBrien, Richard P. *What Do We Really Believe?* Denville, NJ: Dimension Books, 1977.

_____ *Catholicism*. New York: HarperCollins, 1994.

Miles, Jack. *God*. New York: Alfred A. Knopf, 1995.

O'Collins, Gerald S.J., and Mary Venturini, *Believing and Understanding the Creed*. New York: Paulist Press, 1991.

O'Murchu, Diarmuid. *Quantum Theology: Spiritual Implications of the New Physics*. New York: Crossroad, 1997.

Perry, John Michael. *Exploring the Genesis Creation and Fall Stories*. Kansas City, MO: Sheed and Ward, 1992.

_____ *Exploring the Resurrection of Jesus*. Kansas City: Sheed and Ward, 1993.

_____ *Exploring the Identity and Mission of Jesus*. Kansas City: Sheed and Ward, 1996.

Ratzinger, Joseph. *Introduction to Christianity*. Translated by J.R. Foster. New York: Herder and Herder, 1970.

Rahner, Karl, ed. *Sacramentum Mundi: An Encyclopedia of Theology*, 6 volumes. New York: Herder and Herder, 1969.

Schaupp, Joan. *Woman: Image of the Holy Spirit*. Denville, NJ: Dimension Books, 1975.

Thielicke, Helmut. *I Believe: The Christian's Creed*. Translated by John W. Coberstein and H. George Anderson. Philadelphia: Fortress Press, 1968.

Vardey, Lucinda. *God in All Worlds: An Anthology of Contemporary Spiritual Writing*. New York: Vintage, 1995.

Wijngaards, John. *How to Make Sense of God*. Kansas City: Sheed and Ward, 1995.

Wilson, Andrew, ed. *World Scripture: A Comparative Anthology of Sacred Texts*. New York: Paragon House, 1991.

ACKNOWLEDGMENTS

So much of what we believe in life we come to believe because of others. We see in others the kind of commitment it takes to go on believing when our own belief falters. We look to others for the kind of vision that stretches our own beyond the daily. We depend on others for the kind of wisdom that exceeds answers. We hold on to others to find the kind of love that makes life rich with meaning, certain proof of the everlasting love of a God for whom there is no word. Most often, we attribute that kind of influence to family members or teachers, and that is certainly true. But my own experience is that those kinds of people are all around us, as well. We work beside them and live next to them and watch them go about their daily lives with an unbearable but faith-filled sense of the routine. These acknowledgments are an attempt to recognize friends and associates who brought their own witness, their own beliefs, their own questions, to this book. To all of them, I am grateful not just for the help with this project but for the models of faith they bring to my own life.

I am grateful to Patricia A. Kossmann, my editor, for her patience with the process and her clear commitment to the voice of the writer and the questions of the time.

I am grateful, as well, to the people who were willing to read and discuss this material with me with honesty and openness: to Gail Grossman Freyne; Marjorie and Joseph

Eisert; Ann McCarthy, OSB; Kathleen Hartsell Stephens; Rev. Henry Kriegel; Joan Hodges More; Linda Romey, OSB; Dr. Mary Hembrow Snyder; Dorothy Stoner, OSB; Kathleen Cribbins, OSB; Rev. Thomas Suppa; and Ann Teed. Every reader brought more to the manuscript than simply a concern for the editorial niceties of style. They each brought the kind of sincerity of search and honest concerns that prodded the manuscript to new levels of integrity.

I am grateful, too, for the staff that works with me from one end of a manuscript to another with precision, with honesty, and with a commitment far beyond any semblance of the forty-hour week. Without Marlene Bertke, OSB, Mary Lee Farrell, GNSH, and Mary Grace Hanes, OSB, this work, whatever its meaning, would never have made it to final form. I am always mindful in a special way of the unsparing support, the caring concern and the extra hours of administration given by Maureen Tobin, OSB, that makes all these long periods of writing possible for me.

I am grateful to Mary Ann Longo, RSM, and the staff of Our Lady of the Pines Retreat Center in Fremont, Ohio, who gave me the hermitage and protected the privacy I needed to produce this work.

Finally, I am grateful to the number of readers, listeners, seekers, who have been willing to share with me the reluctance they feel to say the Creed. Without them, this book would never have been written. Without them, I myself may never have taken time to think all of these things through again so thoroughly. I will be forever grateful.

Most of all, I am grateful for those people in my life who taught me not only to ask questions but to wait with total trust in an ever-revealing God who through the very process of living makes so many of the answers, not clear, perhaps, but in the long run, essentially unimportant.

ABOUT THE AUTHOR

J oan Chittister, international author and lecturer, is
founder and director of Benetvision, a research and
resource center for contemporary spirituality. She is
past prioress of the Benedictine Sisters of Erie (PA) and past
president of the Leadership Conference of Women Religious.
She is a social psychologist with a doctorate in speech-com-
munication theory from Penn State. The recipient of many
awards for her work for justice, peace, and equality in the
Church, she has written numerous popular books including
*WomanStrength: Modern Church, Modern Women; A Pas-
sion for Life: Fragments of the Face of God; In a High Spiritual Season; Heart of Flesh: A Feminist Spirituality for
Women and Men;* and *The Fire in These Ashes: A Spirituality of Contemporary Religious Life.* She lives in Erie, Pennsylvania.